THE PAINTER, GILDER, AND VARNISHER'S COMPANION

PHILADELPHIA
HENRY CAREY BAIRD
1850

The Toolemera Press
History Preserved
toolemerapress.com

The Painter, Gilder, And Varnisher's Companion: Henry Carey Baird; Philadelphia, 1850

No part of this book may be reproduced, stored in an electronic retrieval system, or transmitted in any form or by an means, electronic, mechanical, photocopy, photographic or otherwise without the written permission of the publisher.

Excerpts of one page or less for the purposes of review and comment are permissible.

Copyright © 2010 The Toolemera Press
All rights reserved.

International Standard Book Number
ISBN : 978-0-9825329-4-2 (Trade Paperback)

Published by
Gary Roberts DBA Toolemera Press
Wilmington, North Carolina
U.S.A. 28401

THE PAINTER, GILDER, AND VARNISHER'S COMPANION:

CONTAINING

RULES AND REGULATIONS

IN

EVERYTHING RELATING TO THE ARTS OF PAINTING,
GILDING, VARNISHING, AND GLASS-STAINING:

NUMEROUS USEFUL AND VALUABLE RECEIPTS;
TESTS FOR THE DETECTION OF ADULTERATIONS IN OILS, COLOURS, &C.

AND A

STATEMENT OF THE DISEASES AND ACCIDENTS TO WHICH PAINTERS,
GILDERS, AND VARNISHERS ARE PECULIARLY LIABLE;

WITH THE SIMPLEST AND BEST METHODS OF
PREVENTION AND REMEDY.

PHILADELPHIA:
HENRY C. BAIRD, successor to E. L. CAREY.
1850.

Entered according to the act of Congress, in the year 1850, by
HENRY C. BAIRD,
in the Clerk's Office of the District Court for the Eastern District of Pennsylvania.

PHILADELPHIA:
T. K. AND P. G. COLLINS, PRINTERS.

PREFACE.

The object of the "PAINTER, GILDER, AND VARNISHER'S COMPANION" is to give a clear, concise, and comprehensive view of the principal operations connected with the practice of those trades; and to embody, in as little compass and as simple language as possible, the present state of knowledge in the arts of Painting, Gilding, and Varnishing, including all the information derived from the numerous recent discoveries in Chemistry. It has been the compiler's aim, while he has rejected all that appeared foreign to the subject, to omit nothing of real utility; and he trusts he shall be found to have attained it.

The best authorities have been consulted throughout, and the arrangement has been uniformly made with a view to practical purposes. The names of the different substances mentioned are those in common use; and wherever it has been found necessary to employ a term not generally known, an explanation has been given in a note or otherwise.

In the receipts, accuracy has been carefully attended

to in stating the number and the nature of the ingredients to be employed, and the fullest and plainest instructions given for the proper methods of applying them.

The arts of Polishing, Waxing, Lacquering, Japanning, &c., being intimately connected with the trades of Painting, Gilding, and Varnishing, are properly introduced in the following pages. Receipts are likewise given for the preparation of Sail Cloth, Oil Cloth, Printer's Ink, Court Plaster, and a variety of other substances, the composition of which, depending upon operations rendered familiar to the Painter, Gilder, or Varnisher, by his ordinary occupation, will make these additions both useful and interesting to him.

The reader will also find an account of the principal adulterations practiced upon oils, colours, gums, &c., with the readiest modes of detecting them.

The numerous accidents and peculiar diseases to which Painters, Gilders, and Varnishers are known to be liable in the exercise of their trade, have suggested to me the propriety of introducing a notice of the chief of these, with their general causes, and pointing out the best means of prevention and remedy. For the information contained on this head, I am indebted to the kind assistance of a medical gentleman of extensive acquirements and great experience.

I trust it is needless to observe that I do not profess, in the following pages, to instruct the experienced Painter, Gilder, or Varnisher in his business; but I flatter myself that even he may find in them something that is either new to him or which he has as yet known but imperfectly or incorrectly. There was a time when persons engaged in mechanical trades distrusted everything in the way of their business, except what they had themselves seen or practiced. But this state of things has gone by, and, together with the ignorance and prejudice that occasioned it, has been banished by the general thirst after knowledge at present so prevalent. Every mechanic is now aware that his experience alone can supply him with no facts beyond the limits of his particular observation and practice; while, in perusing a well-executed treatise on his art, he is enabled to combine the experience and observation of other persons with his own, and to profit by them accordingly.

It is presumed that the "PAINTER, GILDER, AND VARNISHER'S COMPANION" may be useful to others besides professed tradesmen. Persons happening to reside at a distance from any regular tradesman, or who, possessing confined means or ample leisure, wish to execute light work of this nature themselves, will find the present treatise a material assistance to them. And even to gentlemen differently circumstanced it may be extremely serviceable, by enabling them, when they have workmen engaged in painting and gilding on an extensive scale, to superintend and direct the operations of those they employ, and, in many cases, to judge of their integrity and ability.

THE PAINTER, GILDER, AND VARNISHER'S COMPANION.

TOOLS AND APPARATUS.

Before proceeding to enter upon any details respecting the nature, use, and composition of the substances employed by the Painter, Gilder, and Varnisher, I shall give a description of the tools and apparatus necessary in these occupations, with directions for their selection and proper use. The first in order and in importance are the *grindstone* and *muller*, employed in grinding colours. The grindstone in common use is a horizontal slab, about eighteen inches square, and sufficiently heavy to enable it to remain fixed and firm, while the colours are ground upon it. The best material is spotted marble or granite; but when that cannot be procured without inconvenience or great expense, white or black marble may be used. Particular care must be taken that the stone is hard and of a close grain, and not full of small pores, which will be sure to retain part of the colours first ground, and thus prevent the stone from being properly cleaned, and render the colours that are ground afterwards mixed and dingy.

A large piece of slate is sometimes used for a grindstone; but this is very improper, except where the colours are quite of a common description and the painting requires no nicety.

The *muller* is a pebble-stone, in the shape of an egg, with the larger end broken off, and then ground as smooth and flat as possible. It is generally to be purchased ready-made at the colour shops. The greater its size (if the dimensions are not so large as to make it difficult for the workman, with a moderate exertion of the strength of his arms, to keep it in continual motion) the better. The usual size is from two to three inches in diameter at the flat end, and about five inches high. In choosing it, the principal points to be observed are, that the surface is perfectly smooth and the edges well rounded off.

An excellent substitute for the common grindstone and muller, but confined in its application to the grinding of colours in a dry state, has been invented by Mr. Charles Taylor, of Manchester, England, and is represented by Figs. 1 and 2.

Fig. 1 represents a mortar, made of marble or other hard stone. One made in the usual form will answer.

M is a muller or grinder, made nearly in the form of a pear, in the upper part of which an iron axis is firmly fixed; which axis, at the parts marked N, N, turns in grooves or slits, made in two pieces of oak, projecting

TAYLOR'S INDIGO GRINDING-MILL.

Fig. 1.   Fig. 2.

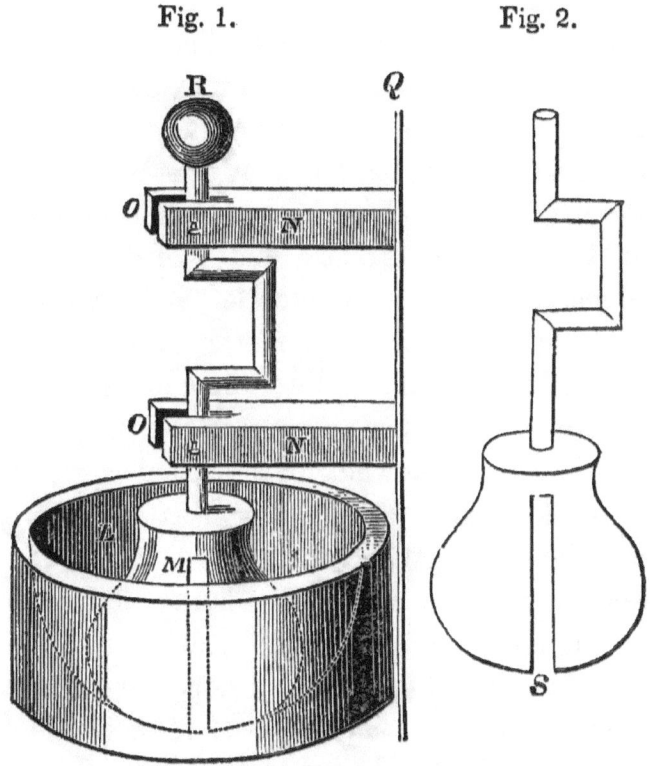

horizontally from a wall, &c.; and when the axis is at work, it is secured in the grooves by the iron pins O, O.

P, the handle, which forms a part of the axis, and by turning which the grinder is worked.

Q, the wall, &c., in which the oak pieces, N, N, are fixed.

R, a weight, which may occasionally be added, if more power is wanted.

Fig. 2 shows the muller or grinder with its axis separate from the other machinery: its bottom should be made to fit the mortar.

S, a groove cut through the stone muller.

The muller being placed in the mortar, and secured in the oak pieces by means of the pins, the colour to be ground is thrown into the mortar, above the muller; on turning the handle, the colour in lumps falls into the groove cut through the muller; and is from thence drawn in under the action of the muller, and again propelled to its outer edge, within the mortar; from whence the coarser particles again fall into the groove of the muller, and are again ground underneath it; this operation is continued until the whole of the colour is ground to an impalpable powder: the muller is then readily removed and the colour taken out.

To prevent any of the colour from flying off in dust under the rapid operation of the muller, and to save also the workmen from inhaling any of those pernicious matters which enter into the composition of most paints, a wooden cover, made in two halves, with a hole in it for the axis of the muller to pass through, is usually placed on the mortar while at work. Had Mr. Taylor's mill nothing else to recommend it, the protection which it thus affords to the health of the workmen ought alone to insure its general adoption. The common grindstone and muller are, in this respect, particularly objectionable. For mixing, or rather perfectly incorporating, colours, after they are dry-ground, with oil or water, and still farther refining them, recourse may be had to the mill for which Mr. Rawlinson, artist, in England, received a prize from the Society of Arts.

RAWLINSON'S INDIGO GRINDING-MILL.

Fig. 3.

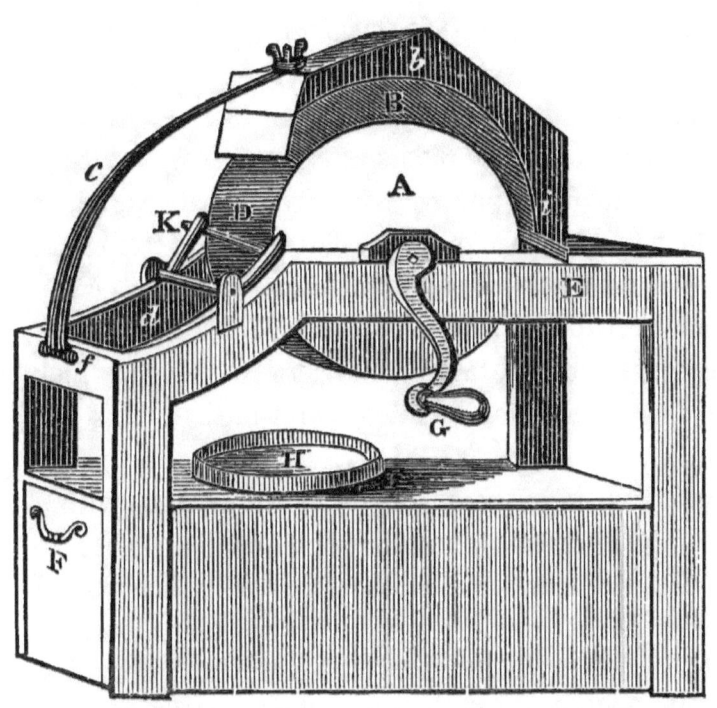

A is a cylinder, made of any kind of marble; but black marble is esteemed the best, because it is the hardest, and takes the best polish. B is a concave muller, covering one-third of the circumference of the cylinder, and made of the same kind of marble with it: this is fixed in a wooden frame, *b*, which is hung to the frame E at *i*, *i*. *c* is a piece of iron, about an inch broad, to keep the muller steady; and is affixed to the frame by a joint at *f*. The small binding screw (with its nut)

which passes through the centre of the iron plate *c*, is for the purpose of laying more pressure on the muller when required, as well as to keep it steady. D is a taker-off, made of a piece of clock-spring, about half an inch broad; and is fixed, similarly to a frame-saw, in an iron frame, K, in an inclined position to the cylinder; and the frame turns on pivots at *d, d*. G is a sliding-board, made to draw out occasionally in order to clean it, should any particles of paint fall upon it from the cylinder; it also forms a support for the dish H, to catch the colour as it drops from the taker-off D. F is a drawer for the purpose of containing curriers' shavings, which are the best things for cleaning paint-mills. E is the mill frame.

The colour being mixed with oil or water, and, with a spatula or palette-knife, put upon the cylinder near to the top of the concave muller, the cylinder is then turned round towards the muller; which draws the colour beneath the muller without any difficulty; and a very few turns of the cylinder spread it equally over the surface. When it is found to be ground sufficiently fine for the purpose required, it is very readily removed by means of the taker-off before described; which must be held against the cylinder and the cylinder be turned the reverse way, which cleans it very quickly and completely; and the muller will only require to be cleaned when the operation is nearly completed and previous to changing the colour. For this purpose, it is to be turned back, being, as before said, hung upon pivots affixed to the frame at *i, i;* and may then be very conveniently cleaned with a palette-knife or a spatula. Afterwards, a handful of the curriers' shavings being held upon the cylinder, by two or three revolutions it is cleaned effectually; and there is much less waste of colour with this machine than with any marble slab.

For the purpose of clearing the colour off the common grinding-stone, as well as for keeping it together should it spread too much during the grinding, painters sometimes employ a piece of horn, like that used for lanterns, about three inches by four, or a piece of wood of the same dimensions, very thin and smooth, and made sharp and even at the edge. This is called a *voider*. It is, however, more customary to use for this purpose a *palette-knife*. This instrument is commonly sold in the shops, and is generally made of steel, which ought to be highly tempered, extremely thin, and perfectly flexible. Ivory, however, is a much preferable material for the palette-knife; since some kinds of yellows assume a dingy, dark green hue, and all colours which contain any portion of arsenic in their composition experience a change when touched with iron or steel.

In no particular ought the painter or varnisher, who wishes to insure superiority in the execution of his work, to be more circumspect than in the choice of his *brushes* and *pencils*.

Brushes are either round or flat, and are of various sizes. The round ones vary from a quarter of an inch to two inches and a half in diameter. For some particular purposes they even exceed this latter size. The larger ones are made use of in laying on the first coat of paint, or *priming,* as it is called, and in painting over large surfaces which require considerable quantities of colour. The smaller brushes are for parts, to which, from their size or situation, the large ones cannot be applied. Brushes of a *flat* form are usually termed varnishing brushes, being chiefly used for that purpose; but they are likewise employed in drawing lines, veining, and imitations of variegated woods.

A correspondent of the *Mechanics' Magazine* (vol. i. p. 279) makes an objection to the use of round brushes, which must be allowed to have considerable weight. "Being made round," he says, "they are by no means well adapted in that shape for laying on a flat surface; the consequence is, that painters invariably use their brushes but one way, for the very purpose of wearing them flat, which goes to prove the necessity of an alteration in their general shape." He then describes one which he made with a flat handle, and found to answer much better, for all common purposes, than the ordinary round brush. The handle was of beech, about an inch and a half wide and three-eighths of an inch thick, and, near the end on which the hairs were tied, was beveled off to a thin edge.

Brushes are almost always made of hogs' bristles. Sometimes they are of badger's or goat's hair; especially when required for varnishing fine works with a thin varnish. In choosing them, observe, in the first place, that the hairs are strong; and next, that they are close together, and fast bound with the threads that tie them round in the stocks. If the hairs are weak, the colour will never lie in a good body; if they are not close together, they will spread and divide unequally when used, and consequently cannot work well. But the worst fault of all is, their not being fast bound in the stocks; for, in that case, some of them will come out while you are working, and the appearance of the work will be strangely disfigured by loose hairs being seen buried in the colouring when dry.

Even when as tightly bound together as possible, the hairs often get loose, from the practice so common with painters of keeping their brushes in water when out of use, by which the strings that bind them, though usually glued over, soon become rotten. To prevent brushes from being damaged in this way, get them bound in the usual way, but not glued over, and then work in rosin and grease, which will resist the water, and keep the brush for a long time tight and sound. When by long use the hairs of a good brush begin to work loosely, drive a few thin wedges of wood inside the thread with which they are bound round, and this will render the whole fast again.

Pencils differ from brushes in the smallness of their size and in being manufactured of a much finer and softer hair. In some cases, the hair of the marten, or of children, and even swansdown, are used for them; but these are generally confined to pencils intended for artists, the mechanical painter being rarely engaged in work of such a delicate nature as to require them. Pencils are invariably of a round form. The smallest are fitted into the barrels of quills, the larger sort into tin cases, both placed at the ends of sticks; some of a very large size are fastened into stocks in the same manner as brushes.

In choosing pencils, a very simple trial will prove whether they are fit for your purpose. You have only to put them into your mouth, and, after wetting them a little, draw them out between your tongue and upper lip. Then, if they present a sharp point, and the hairs come out full next to the case, and without separating, the pencils are good: if the hairs show ragged, or are thin at the opposite end to the point, they cannot be depended upon. The sharpness of the point is of particular consequence in small pencils. The same attention must be paid to the hairs being fast bound in the stocks or cases, as directed in the choice of brushes.

With regard to the stick, or stock, attached to the pencil, it ought never to be *less* than eight inches; and, indeed, the greater the length, provided the workman can handle it with freedom and certainty, the better; for it is as impossible for a painter to have a good command of his pencil, as a writer of his pen, if he hold it too near the point.

To steady the hand while using the pencil, painters use what they call a *moll-stick*. This is made of a straight piece of wood, generally mahogany, with a nob at one end of it, resembling a printer's puff, but smaller, composed of some soft substance enclosed in leather. This end must be rested lightly on the work and the other end being held in the left hand, will render the stick a support to the right.

When you are engaged upon works which will require the use of pencils or small brushes for a long time together, it is customary, instead of having your colours in pots or pans, to dispose them in such quantities as they are likely to be wanted in, upon a *palette*. This is a small board, generally of an oval form, to be had at any colour-shop. It ought to be made of walnut or apple-tree wood, and, before being used, it should be well rubbed over with drying oil, till it refuses to take up any more. The same kind of palette will serve for the varnisher; but, for painting in distemper, it is necessary to have one made of tin-plate.

Spatulas, resembling in appearance the spreading slices used by apothecaries, are useful for preparing colors, and for many other purposes. They should be had of different materials, horn, bone, iron, steel, or ivory; but there should be at least one of each of the last two kinds, those made of steel being sometimes improper, for the reason mentioned in speaking of the palette-knife.

A *glass mattrass* is usually recommended for digesting varnishes, as its transparency admits of the progress of the solution being readily observed. But it is only the experienced manipulator who can safely employ a vessel of this kind; and for general use one of tin is much better.

A *rubber*, for varnishing or polishing, is usually made by rolling up a strip of thick woollen-cloth, which has been torn off so as to form a soft elastic edge; thick wide list will, however, answer equally well. The coil may be from one to three inches in diameter, according to the size of the work.

There are other articles which it may be desirable, or even indispensable, for the painter, gilder, or varnisher to have among his apparatus, but which do not require any description of their nature or use, or any directions for their selection—such as putty,* a putty-knife, dusting-cloths and brushes, pots and pans of different sizes, made of tin or earthenware, to hold colours, (when of earthenware they should be glazed), a large pestle and mortar, hair and silk-sieves, square and rule, compasses, and black-lead pencils.

* Putty is made of common whiting, pounded very fine, and mixed up with linseed oil, till it becomes about the thickness of dough.

COLOURS.

I shall now proceed to mention the principal colouring substances, with their combinations, pointing out their comparative advantages and disadvantages. In a few instances, where the process is not tedious or difficult, or where there would be a risk of getting them in a very impure state at the shops, I shall state the method of preparing them for use. In most cases, particularly since the general erection of colour-mills, it will be found a saving both of time and expense to purchase them ready prepared.

WHITES.

White Lead, Ceruse, and Flake White.

The white colour most generally used in house-painting, and which forms the best priming for all other colors, is a subcarbonate of lead, consisting of 85 parts of pure lead and 25 of carbonic acid. The more common sorts are called *white lead*; the purer, *ceruse*; the very best, *flake white*. The following is a simple and expeditious method of preparing it.

Take some long narrow slips of lead, and make them up into rolls, leaving a small space between every fold, so that none of the surfaces may touch one another anywhere; place these rolls in earthen pots, upheld by a little bar in such a manner as not to sink down above half way into the pots; and in each of these vessels put as much strong vinegar as nearly to touch the lead. When the vinegar and the lead are both in the pot, cover it up close, and leave it under the action of a moderate heat, till the plates of lead are reduced to a complete calx, which when dried will become very solid. If you find that the process has not been continued long enough, knock off the part of the surface of the lead which is calcined, and repeat the process with the remainder.

When cakes of white lead are purchased ready prepared, small particles of lead in the metallic state are not unfrequently found, owing to the preparation having been imperfectly executed; and in grinding the colour, this metallic part, becoming divided by the motion of the muller, gives a grayish tint to it. To avoid this inconvenience, if you do not prepare your white lead yourself, be careful to ascertain as well as you can, in purchasing it, whether it is pure, and select the thinnest cakes. In grinding it, your slab and muller should be perfectly clean; because there is often a little acid moisture in white lead, which renders it very apt to attract any parts that remain of colours previously ground. To obtain white lead of a very fine quality, it is often necessary to grind it several times.

Not unfrequently this colour is adulterated with common whiting, and its beauty by this means greatly impaired. To detect this fraud, rub a little of the suspected article between the fingers, and throw it on a piece of live charcoal; if pure, the *whole* of it will turn of a yellowish hue, and in a few minutes take the form of brilliant metallic globules; but if any whiting has been mixed with it, there will be a corresponding residue of a white earthy appearance.

Spanish, or Bougival, White.

A precipitate, formed by the solutions of bismuth when thrown into water, is what goes, in commerce, by the name of Spanish White, Bougival White (from Bougival, near Marly in France), and sometimes White of Bismuth. It is generally sold in cakes of an oblong form. It is much better for house-painting than any whites that contain a mixture of chalky substances, and it is not unfrequently used instead of white lead for priming, being far cheaper, though much less durable. When employed with oil or varnish, it ought to be used very dry, or it will unite but imperfectly with them.

Rolls of washed chalk, possessing none of the qualities that should belong to Spanish or Bougival White, are often sold under these names. To detect this adulteration, pour upon the sample a few drops of aqua fortis, or very strong distilled vinegar. If the Spanish White be pure, no effervescence will take place; if any effervescence appears, it is either wholly or in part chalk.

Gypsum, or Plaster of Paris.

Gypsum is a sulphate of lime, composed of lime and sulphuric acid. It requires to be calcined before it is used as a colouring substance. When employed in house-painting, it requires to be mixed with a great quantity of water, and it then forms a very valuable article for white-washing apartments, and for painting in distemper. Its white, when the gypsum is quite pure and free from any mixture of clay, is very fine, and much more delicate than that of chalk.

White of Troyes, or White Chalk.

The substance known by these names is an insoluble compound formed of carbonic acid and lime. It is generally used for common white-washing; though gypsum is much preferable for this purpose. In distemper it answers very well, as its being mixed up with size renders it more durable; but with oil and varnishes it becomes brown, and occasions the latter to split. Like all colours that contain chalk, it is without lustre.

BLACKS.

Ivory Black.

The bones of all animals, when reduced to charcoal or carbon, form a good black; but the best of all blacks, whether animal or vegetable, is that made from ivory shavings burnt to a black coal, in a crucible closely stopped up, and afterwards ground very fine. It may be freed from every possible impurity by washing it in muriatic acid or weak aqua-fortis, and is then an extremely rich and intense color; but being costly, it is seldom employed in common work. The water colour, called *China Ink*, is merely ivory black perfectly pure, mixed with a solution of isinglass and Spanish liquorice, and then evaporated to a proper consistence.

Lamp Black.

The soot collected by holding a plate over the flame of a lamp or candle is the veritable lamp black; but the more general way of obtaining this substance on a large scale is from the burning of resinous woods. It is used more than any other black in common painting. It serves to modify the brightness of the tints of other colours, and is very useful in the composition of such colours as result from mixtures. It is both cheap and plentiful; is a very good black for general purposes; and of so fine a body that, if tempered only with linseed oil, it will serve, on most occasions, to work without grinding. But as the substance of this colour contains a kind of greasy fatness, which makes it long in drying, it is advisable to mix two parts of drying oil with the linseed oil, or to grind some white copperas and mix it with the colour, which will make it dry in a short time. Its unctuosity may be also greatly lessened, and its lustre at the same time much improved, by burning it in a crucible or iron ladle made red-hot over a clear fire.

Charcoal Blacks.

The best charcoal is that procured by subjecting wood, enclosed in a cast-iron cylinder and wholly excluded from the action of the air, to a strong fire till the cylinder is red-hot. The whole of the gaseous ingredients being then disengaged, the fire is extinguished and the charcoal allowed to cool in the cylinder. The woods that furnish the best charcoal for painters are the beech and vine; the former yielding a black of a bluish, and the latter one of a grayish, cast. *Wine Lees*, after being calcined, washed several times in boiling water, and ground to a fine powder, yield a fine velvety black, which, however, is chiefly used by copper-plate printers. *Peach Stones*, burned in a close vessel, yield a charcoal which, after being ground, may be successfully used for that kind of black generally known by the name of *raven gray*. A very pure charcoal is also obtained by exposing white sugar-candy to a red heat in an earthenware retort. When charcoal obtained from any of these sources is employed in painting, it should be mixed with a very small portion of white lead, and made up for use with drying oil.

REDS.

Vermilion.

The most delicate and brilliant of all the light reds is that called *Vermilion*, obtained from the red sulphuret, commonly known by the name of *cinnabar*. Although cinnabar is found in a natural state, being the ore from which mercury is usually extracted, it is, in general, prepared artificially, when vermilion is intended to be manufactured out of it. The process is simple. Melt six ounces of sulphur in an iron ladle; then put two pounds of mercury into a chamois leather, or a double linen cloth, and squeeze it thence into the melted brimstone, stirring them at the same time with a wooden spatula, till they are well combined, forming a substance the same as the natural cinnabar. When the mass is cold, beat it into a powder, and sublime it in a glass vessel with a worm-like top, over a strong fire; when the ascending fumes will form an incrustation on the top of the vessel, which, reduced to a fine powder, is vermilion.

The body of vermilion is very delicate, and will grind as fine as oil itself. No colour looks better, works smoother, bears a better body, or goes farther.

It is not unfrequently debased by a mixture of red lead. To detect this adulteration, place a portion of it on a piece of red-hot iron: if pure, it will evaporate entirely; if not, there will be an earthy residue.

Minium, or Red Lead.

This colour is made by first reducing common lead, by calcining, to an oxide or litharge, which being ground to powder, is put into a hot furnace exposed to a free access of air, and continually stirred with an iron rake, till the colour becomes a fine pale red.

The grinding red lead to a proper degree of fineness is very laborious and difficult, it being naturally very harsh and sandy. When, however, it is well ground and made fine, it is lighter than any other red in general use, bears a good body in oil, and binds very fast, and firm. It has likewise the advantage of drying readily.

Carmine.

A more dazzling red than vermilion (the superfine species of it, called *Madame Cenette's*, is almost too brilliant for the eye to endure) is derived from the precipitation of the colouring matter in cochineal, by means of an acid—usually alum. Various sorts of carmine are sold at the colour-shops, and numbered in the order of their relative value: thus, No. 1 is the best; No. 2, the second best; and so on. Some modes of manufacturing it may be superior to others, but the difference of quality arises chiefly from an excess of alum employed in the precipitation, or from the intermixture of a portion of vermilion. In the first case, the colour is weakened; in the second, it does not retain the same brilliancy. It is always easy to detect the proportion of mixture, by means of a property which pure carmine possesses of dissolving in ammonia. All the *foreign* matters remain untouched, and the proportion they bear may be estimated by drying the residuum.

The preparation of this article is involved in considerable mystery, for in consequence of the great cost of the original material, cochineal, the consumption of it is limited, and the manufacture confined to a few hands. There are many receipts for the purpose in scientific books, but success appears to depend on a certain dexterity, which habit alone can confer. One of the *likeliest* processes seems to me to be the following :—

Boil one pound of powdered cochineal and three and a half drachms of subcarbonate of potash, in ten gallons of water, checking the effervescence from time to time, by adding a little cold water. When the mixture has boiled for some minutes, take the boiler off the fire and place it on a table, so inclined that the liquor may be easily poured off. Now throw in eight drachms of alum in powder, and stir the whole well, when the decoction will instantly assume a very brilliant tint. In about a quarter of an hour the cochineal, divested of its colouring matter, will be seen deposited at the bottom, and the liquor as clear as if it had been filtered. Draw off this liquor into another boiler; and after adding three and a half drachms of isinglass dissolved in water and passed through a sieve, set it on the fire. As soon as it begins to boil, the carmine will be seen rising to the surface of the bath, and a coagulum will be formed, similar to that which takes place in the clarifications made with whites of eggs. The boiler must then be withdrawn from the fire, and the bath well stirred with a spatula; in fifteen or twenty minutes after which, the carmine will have all fallen to the bottom. The clear fluid is then poured off, and the precipitate laid to drain on a very fine sieve. If the whole of this process has been properly performed, the carmine, when dry, will easily break between the fingers.

Lake.

There are two sorts of colours known under this name; lakes derived foom cochineal—the richest and finest of all dark reds; and lakes prepared from madder—not quite so good.

Cochineal lake is obtained by boiling the fluid which remains after the precipitation of the carmine in the manner described under the preceding head, along with potashes and the deposit which was left in the boiler after the addition of the alum. When all the heavier matters have fallen to the bottom, the clear fluid is drawn off and alum again added. A precipitate is then thrown down, which when drained and dried is *cochineal lake*.

Madder lakes—or, as they are sometimes called, *madder carmine*—are nearly as costly as cochineal lakes, and not so *much* inferior as is generally supposed. They are very durable, and have the peculiar merit of long retaining an appearance of great freshness. Madder being itself abundant and cheap, the costliness of madder lakes has been hitherto entirely owing to the extremely tedious and complicated methods pursued in the manufacturing of them; but in consequence of certain scientific researches recently entered into by Messrs. Colin and Roubiquet (see *Annales de Chim.*, March, 1827), so much light has been thrown on the subject, that the same results may now be obtained in three or four hours only, which formerly required several successive months; and that too, in a very simple manner. "The manipulations," say Messrs. Colin and Roubiquet, "are so easy in practice, that it is in every person's power to undertake them; and in a little time, we have no doubt, the use of these lakes will extend to the commonest objects."

The new mode consists in mixing one part of madder with four parts of water, leaving it to macerate for ten minutes only, and then submitting it to a powerful pressure, till nearly every portion of liquid is squeezed out. Three times this process is repeated; and to the washing liquor preserved in each instance, there is added five or six parts more of pure water, and half a pint of pounded alum. The mixture is then allowed to macerate for two or three hours, in the heat of a water bath, and stirred occasionally with a spatula. It is next strained through a fine cloth, and afterwards filtered through paper. A dilute solution of crystals of soda is finally added, when a precipitate is formed, which is the colouring matter wanted. Messrs. Colin and Roubiquet recommend that the dilute solution of crystals of soda should be divided into three portions; by which means three precipitates will be obtained, decreasing successively in colour and richness.

Spanish Brown.

This is obtained from an earth dug out of the ground: it is of a dark dull red colour, something like horse-flesh. The deeper the colour, and the freer from gritty particles, the better it is for use. It is cheap and plentiful, and works well. It is much employed by painters for a priming, or first colour.

Other Reds.

Besides the above reds, I may mention among those in use among painters, *English red* and *Prussian red*, both obtained from oxides of iron, and commonly called colcothar of vitriol; *red ochre*, which is very extensively employed, especially in distemper; *rose colour*, composed of a portion of white lead mixed with pure lake; and *realgar*, which is formed of fifty-eight parts of arsenic and forty-two of sulphur.

YELLOWS.

Yellow Ochre.

Of this colour there are two kinds, the *bright yellow* and the *dark yellow*. The former is sometimes called *plain ochre*, and the latter *spruce ochre*. It will grind very fine, resists the weather well, and bears a good body.

Massicot.

The substance known under this name in commerce is produced by the calcination of lead in contact with the air; it is the lead, in fact, in its first state of change, after being combined with the oxygen of the atmosphere; heated a little longer, it is converted into minium, or red lead; longer still, into a brown oxide, which is of no use in the arts. It is a good light yellow for general purposes, and very serviceable, when mixed with blue, for making greens.

Chrome Yellow.

The mineral called chrome, discovered by M. Vauquelin, in 1797, was so called from the peculiar property it possesses of colouring whatever it combines with—*chrome* signifying *colour.* Of the various compound colours of which it is the basis, the most valuable is that called *chrome yellow,* or *chromate of lead,* obtained by pouring a solution of chromate of potass into a solution of any of the salts of lead. It is a very rich and brilliant yellow, and employed to advantage in house and coach painting. To test its purity, pour a little nitric acid upon it: if it effervesces, it is adulterated.

Turner's, or Patent Yellow.

When sea-salt is made into a paste with litharge, it is decomposed, its acid unites with the litharge, and the soda is set free. Hence Turner's patent process for decomposing sea-salt, which consists in mixing two parts of the former with one of the latter, moistening them, and leaving them together for about twenty-four hours. The product is then washed, filtered, and evaporated, by which soda is obtained. A white substance is now left undissolved; it is a compound of muriatic acid and lead, which, when heated, changes its colour, and forms *Tur-*

ner's Yellow—a very beautiful colour, much in use among coach painters.

Orpiment.

This colour is more commonly known by the name of *yellow arsenic*. It is a compound of about fifty-eight parts of arsenic and forty-two of sulphur. It is good for some purposes, particularly for the production of straw colours in painting doors, windows, &c.; but as it is a stony substance, the grinding of it is a very difficult, and, from its poisonous nature, an injurious operation. It likewise, in common with all bodies that contain arsenic, produces a bad effect on any metallic substances exposed to its action.

Naples Yellow.

The best of all yellows: it is milder and more unctuous than either orpiment, massicot, or any of the ochres; combines readily with other colours, and improves them. It is generally supposed to be obtained from the lava of Mount Vesuvius; but M. de Bondaroy says (*Memoirs of the French Academy*, 1766) that it is a composition known at Naples under the name of *giallolini*, the mode of preparing which is known only to one individual. On afterwards analyzing it, he found it to consist of ceruse, alum, sal-ammoniac, and diaphoretic antimony. It is necessary to use it with great care. It must be ground well on a slab of porphyry or marble, and scraped together with an ivory knife, as both stone and steel have a tendency to turn it to green. Sometimes it is adulterated by an intermixture of iron; to detect this, fuse a portion of it along with colourless glass: if free from iron, it will become of a milk-white colour.

Yellow of Antimony.

A yellow obtained from dissolving crude antimony in muriatic acid holds an intermediate place between chrome yellow and Naples yellow. It is chiefly used for giving a yellow colour to glass and earthenware.

Yellow Pink.

A variety of yellow colours are also obtained from vegetable substances. The most durable of these is that extracted from the *reseda luteola*, a plant common to most European countries. It grinds and dissolves in water easily; but care must be taken not to bring it in contact with iron, as the astringent principle which it contains in abundance, instantly dissolves that metal, which in its turn destroys the clearness of the colour.

BLUES.

Prussian Blue.

A Prussian chemist, when making experiments on iron happened to pour a solution of one of its salts on a solution of potashes which had been kept for some time on animal matter, and found that a blue substance was formed. Following up the hint thus accidentally obtained, he succeeded, after a number of experiments, in discovering a method of preparing the valuable colour called *Prussian Blue*. The process, which was long kept secret, is as follows: Four parts of bullock's blood, dried by the application of a slight heat, are mixed with an equal weight of potashes, and again exposed to a strong heat till the fumes which are at first given off cease to appear. The residue is then boiled in about twelve quarts of water, and strained, and to the solution are added two parts of green vitriol, and eight of alum. A blue powder is now deposited, which is to be washed by muriatic acid, and then dried. There are blue colours superior to this, both in clearness and durability; but none which, volume for volume, contains so large a quantity of colouring matter. M. Bourgeois, a practical colourman, says that it contains even ten to one more than any other colour. It is on this account, much employed in house-painting, and also in colouring paper-hangings. Unfortunately, it is affected by all the alkalis, and therefore is fit for mixing with any colour which contains them. When ground with oil, it takes a yellowish tint; the best method to prevent which is to mix a little lake.

Indigo.

Another blue colour, much used in common painting is *indigo*, extracted from the plant *indigofera*, found in America, Egypt, and the East Indies. None but the best and purest kind of this colour—that obtained from the *indigofera argentea*—is proper for oil painting:

that of an inferior quality is only fit for distemper, as the oil renders it black or green.

Indigo grinds fine, and bears a very good body. Its natural color, however, being very dark, almost indeed approaching to black, it is seldom or never used without a small mixture of white. A preparation from the leaves of the *anillo* is sometimes fraudulently substituted for indigo, but may be at once detected by throwing a piece into the fire; *as genuine indigo will not burn.*

Ultramarine.

Ultramarine is the richest, mellowest, most beautiful and lasting of all blues; but its extravagant price—nearly equal, when pure, to its weight in gold—prevents it being introduced, unless very rarely indeed, into house painting. It is prepared from *lapis lazuli*. A number of pieces of this mineral are made red hot, and thrown into water, to make them pulverize easily; they are then reduced to a fine powder, and made up into a paste with a varnish compounded of resin, wax, and boiled linseed oil. This paste is put into a linen cloth, and repeatedly kneaded with hot water. The first water is thrown away; the second gives ultramarine of the best quality; the third a colour of less value. The best test of the purity of this article is, to throw it into concentrated nitric acid; if adulterated (as it often is), it will be scarcely affected by the acid; if pure, it will lose its colour almost entirely.

Smalt, Zaffre, Azure, Saxon Blue, or Enamel Blue.

A compound known in commerce by all these different names, and bearing a strong resemblance to ultramarine, is obtained by dissolving cobalt in nitric acid, and precipitating it by a solution of potash. It is of a lovely azure hue; but if not bought in the form of powder, is very difficult to grind, and it can be used only in a peculiar manner. It is too sandy to bear any body in oil; besides that oil would change its colour, and make it of a black cast. The only proper, indeed the only practicable, method of laying it on, is by strewing it on a ground of white lead, which is done in the following manner: Temper white lead with good clear drying oil, as stiff as you can well use it with the pencil or brush: with this white cover the surface or the work you intend to strew with smalt, being sure to cover it completely and equally. Then strew your smalt thickly over this white ground, *while it is moist*, and with the feather-edge of a goose-quill stroke it over, that it may lie evenly and thickly alike on all parts, and with a piece of linen cloth dab it down close, that it may take well upon the ground laid under it. When you find the ground quite dry, wipe off the loose colour with a feather, and blow the remainder off with a pair of bellows. A portion of Prussian blue is frequently mixed up with the genuine cobalt; and Prussian blue has been even prepared in such a manner as to be passed off for cobalt, without containing a single particle of that ingredient. The property, however, which Prussian blue possesses, of being discoloured by alkalis, furnishes an easy security against any imposition of this sort. Immerse a piece of the suspected article in clarified lime-water for about an hour; if the water has then assumed a citron hue, and there is an ochrous deposit at the bottom, it is a certain proof of the presence of Prussian blue.

Blue Verditer.

This is a beautiful blue, obtained from the waste nitrate of copper of the refiners, by adding to it a quantity of chalk; but it is only proper for distemper: it does not admit of being used with oil, unless a considerable mixture of white is introduced.

GREENS.

Verdigris.

This is the best simple green, and the one most in use. It is obtained by dissolving common verdigris in distilled vinegar or sour wine, and then proceeding to evaporation and crystallization.

It has a bluish tint; but when lightened by the addition of a little yellow pink, it makes a beautiful grass green. It grinds very fine, and works easily, and in a good body.

When delicate painting is required, the dross, mixed with the common verdigris, makes it improper, and it becomes necessary to use *distilled verdigris*, which can be had at the shops, and is free from all impurities; but it is too expensive for ordinary purposes.

Italian, or Verona Green.

According to Haüy, this is a species of chloride (a combination of chlorine with a metallic or other substance). It is of the same colour as chlorine, which derives its name from the Greek word *chloros*, signifying a yellowish green. It is very durable, and not acted on by acids; but being obtained from an earth, does not incorporate well with oil.

Saxon or Hungary Green.

The colour which bears this name is a carbonate of copper, found in a natural state in the mountains of Saxony and Hungary, mixed with earthy matters, which give it a palish hue.

Scheele's Green.

This colour, called after the celebrated chemist by whom its composition was first made known, is an arsenite of copper obtained in the following manner: A pound of sulphate of copper (blue vitriol) is first dissolved in four pints of water; then a pound of carbonate of potass, dissolved in eight pints of water, is boiled for some time with five ounces of white arsenic; the two solutions are now mixed while hot, and a precipitate produced, which, being well washed and dried, is of a light sea-green colour.

It grinds well with oil, and is in much request for the painting of the cabins of ships.

Schweinfurt Green.

A green which has recently obtained great reputation on the continent, and which is said to surpass Scheele's, both in beauty and splendour, may be obtained, according to Dr. Liebig (*Annales de Chimie*), by the following process: Dissolve in a copper kettle, by heat, one part of verdigris in a sufficient quantity of pure vinegar, and add to it an aqueous solution of white arsenic. A precipitate of dirty green generally forms; but you must add more vinegar, and keep the boiler on the fire till that precipitate disappears, and a perfect amalgamation of the materials takes place. After boiling this compound for some time, a granular precipitate will be formed, of a most beautiful green colour, which has then only to be separated from the liquid, well washed, and dried. Should the colour thus prepared have too blue a shade, boil ten pounds of it in a solution of common potash, over a moderate fire, and it will soon acquire a rich yellow tint.

Brunswick Green.

A colour, thus named, is much used for paper-hangings, and coarse kinds of painting in water-colours. It is prepared as follows: A close earthenware vessel is half filled with copper filings or clippings, and a saturated solution of sal-ammoniac poured over them. It is allowed to stand for a few weeks, by which time the whole of the copper becomes oxidyzed (a muriate of copper). The oxide being then well washed, and slowly dried in the shade, is pure Brunswick green. Two parts of copper and three parts of sal-ammoniac yield six parts of green.

Green Verditer.

This is obtained from the same substance as blue verditer, by a process nearly similar. Without the addition of white lead, or Spanish white, it is unfit for oil painting: and in any way, it is better adapted for distemper. Its colour may be obtained in oil, by mixing two or three parts of verdigris with one of white lead.

Green Lake, or Venetian Emerald.

A very simple mode has recently been discovered, at Venice, of producing a fine unchangeable emerald colour. A quantity of coffee is boiled in river water—if spoiled coffee, so much the better. By means of a proportionate quantity of pure soda, a green precipitate is obtained, which is placed to dry, for six or seven days, upon polished marble, stirring it occasionally, in order that every part may come in contact with the atmosphere, by which the vivacity of the colour is greatly heightened. The green lake obtained by this process is said to have resisted the action of acids, and even the influence of light and moisture.

BROWNS.

Umber.

Umber, or, as it is sometimes called, brown ochre, is an impure native oxide of iron and manganese. It is brought from Umbria, in Italy, whence its name. It is much employed by painters, and is the only *simple* brown in common use. A species of it has been lately brought from Cologne, which is a good deal browner and more transparent than that in common use.

The browns arising from mixture will be mentioned in speaking of compound colours.

New Brown, discovered by Mr. Hatchet.

The celebrated chemist, Mr. Hatchet, has suggested to painters that a simple brown colour, far superior in beauty and intensity to all the browns, whether simple or compound, hitherto known, may be obtained from the prussiate of copper (a combination of prussic acid with copper). The following is the process which he recommends: Dissolve the green muriate of copper in about ten times its weight of distilled or rain water, and add a solution of prussiate of lime, until a complete precipitation is effected. The precipitate is then to be washed with cold water, filtered, and set to dry in the shade.

COMPOUND COLOURS, OR COLOURS ARISING FROM MIXTURE.

The various colours that may be obtained by the mixture of other colours, are innumerable. I only propose here to give the best and simplest modes of preparing those most frequently required.

Compound colours formed by the union of only two colours, are called by painters *virgin tints*.

The smaller the number of colours of which any compound colour is composed, the purer and the richer it will be.

Light Gray is made by mixing white lead with lampblack, using more or less of each material, as you wish to obtain a lighter or a darker colour.

Buff is made from yellow ochre and white lead.

Silver, or Pearl Gray.—Mix white lead, indigo, and a very slight portion of black, regulating the quantities by the shade you wish to obtain.

Flaxen Gray is obtained by a mixture of white lead and Prussian blue, with a small quantity of lake.

Brick colour.—Yellow ochre and red lead, with a little white.

Oak-wood colour.—Three-fourths white lead, and one-fourth part umber and yellow ochre: the proportions of the last two ingredients being determined by the required tints.

Walnut-tree colour.—Two-thirds white lead, and one-third red ochre, yellow ochre, and umber, mixed according to the shade sought. If veining is required, use different shades of the same mixture, and, for the deepest places, black.

Jonquil.—Yellow, pink, and white lead. This colour is only proper for distemper.

Lemon Yellow.—Realgar and orpiment. Some object to this mixture, on account of the poisonous nature of the ingredients. The same colour can be obtained by mixing yellow pink with Naples yellow; but it is then only fit for distemper.

Orange colour.—Red lead and yellow ochre.

Violet colour.—Vermilion, or red lead, mixed with black or blue, and a small portion of white. Vermilion is far preferable to red lead, in mixing this colour.

Purple.—Dark red mixed with violet colour.

Carnation.—Lake and white.

Gold colour.—Massicot, or Naples yellow, with a small quantity of realgar, and a very little Spanish white.

Olive colour.—This may be obtained by various mixtures: black and a little blue mixed with yellow; yellow pink with a little verdigris and lamp-black; or ochre and a small quantity of white—will all produce a kind of olive colour. For distemper, indigo and yellow pink, mixed with white lead or Spanish white, must be used. If veined, it should be done with umber.

Lead colour.—Indigo and white.

Chestnut colour.—Red ochre and black for a dark chestnut. To make it lighter, employ a mixture of yellow ochre.

Light Timber colour.—Spruce ochre, white, and a little umber.

Flesh colour.—Lake, white lead, and a little vermilion.

Light Willow Green.—White mixed with verdigris.

Grass Green.—Yellow pink mixed with verdigris.

An endless variety of greens can be obtained by the mixture of blue and yellow in different proportions, with the occasional addition of white lead.

Stone colour.—White, with a little spruce ochre.

Dark Lead colour.—Black and white, with a little indigo.

Fawn colour.—White lead, stone ochre, and a little vermilion.

Chocolate colour.—Lamp-black and Spanish brown. On account of the fatness of the lamp-black, mix some litharge and red lead.

Portland Stone colour.—Umber, yellow ochre, and white lead.

The variety of shades of brown that may be obtained are nearly as numerous as those of green.

To imitate Mahogany.—Let the first coat of painting be white lead, the second orange, and the last burned umber or sienna; imitating the veins according to your taste and practice.

To imitate Wainscot.—Let the first coat be white, the second half white and half yellow ochre, and the third yellow ochre only. Shadow with umber or sienna.

To imitate Satin Wood.—Take white for your first

coating, light blue for the second, and dark blue or dark green for the third.

OILS.

We come next to speak of the principal oils which are used in the preparation both of colours and varnishes.

Oil of Spike was formerly much more in use than it is at present. It is a volatile oil, and has the advantage of drying more speedily than any of the fat oils; it is also free from any offensive odour. It is, however, generally in a very impure state; and of this painters are so thoroughly convinced, that they have pretty generally renounced it. In all preparations for varnishes, where it is directed to be employed, oil of turpentine, which is much cheaper, can be substituted without any other inconvenience than what may arise from its stronger smell.

Oil of Lavender is principally used by enamellers, to whom it is particularly valuable, from its consistency being such as to prevent the colours that are mixed with it from running. Its property of drying more equally and gradually than perhaps any other oil renders it also of service to the varnisher.

Oil of Poppies has one advantage possessed by no other—that of being perfectly colourless. For this reason a decided preference is given to it for delicate kinds of painting. Being, however, extremely fat, it is liable, unless very old, to the objection of being insufferably tedious in drying.

Nut Oil and *Linseed Oil*, both in very general use,

rank among the fat oils. Their fatness, indeed, is so great, that it is mostly found necessary, before employing them in colouring, to give them a drying quality, which may be done in the following manner: Take three parts of white vitriol, and twelve parts of litharge, and let them be reduced to as fine a powder as possible; then mix them with thirty-two parts of nut or linseed oil, and place the mixture over a fire just brisk enough to keep the oil slightly boiling. Let it continue to boil, till the oil entirely ceases to throw up any scum. Then take the vessel off the fire, and let it stand in a cool place for about three hours, and a sediment, which contains the fattening part of the oil, will be formed at the bottom. Pour off the oil which is above (being careful not to let any of the sediment mix with it) into wide-mouthed bottles. Let it remain a sufficient time to clear itself perfectly, before it is used, and you will find it possessed of the proper drying quality.

Sometimes, when the fire is not kept pretty equal while the boiling is going on, the colour of the oil is affected, so as to render it unfit for delicate painting. To avoid this, some persons tie up the litharge and vitriol, when powdered, in a bag; but, in this case, the quantity of litharge must be doubled. The bag must also be suspended by a piece of packthread to a stick made to rest upon the edges of the vessel, so as to keep the bag at the distance of an inch from the bottom. This method, too, is slower than that of boiling the drying material along with the oil.

In some kinds of work, such as the preparation of

floor-cloths, and painting large figures or ornaments, in which clayey colours are employed, an extraordinary rapidity in drying is sometimes necessary, which could not be procured by using the proportions of drying materials above mentioned. In such cases, it is customary to increase the quantity of litharge in any proportion that may be requisite. On some occasions, the litharge employed has amounted to one-fourth part of the whole quantity of oil.

The process used for giving a drying quality to nut and linseed oil will not do for oil of poppies, which would thereby be deprived of its colourless property, the most valuable one which it possesses.

Many painters consider it a matter of indifference whether nut or linseed oil be employed in colouring, and therefore, for the sake of cheapness, give the preference to the latter. But they labour under a mistake; for these two oils should, by no means, be used indiscriminately. In painting which is allowed to be coarse, or which is sheltered from the effects of the rain and sun, linseed oil will answer the purpose. But where any nicety is required in colouring, in situations exposed to the weather, nut oil only is proper, as it nourishes and develops the colour; whereas linseed oil dissipates and destroys it, and obliges the work to be done afresh in a short time. In painting exposed to weather, persons aware of the impropriety of using linseed oil are sometimes induced to mix a portion of oil of turpentine with nut oil, to save cost; but this mixture has almost as injurious an effect in whitening colour which is exposed to the sun, as pure linseed oil.

I have before said that linseed oil will serve for painting that is not exposed to the rain and sun. This is not, however, the case when a pure white is wanted, for linseed oil has the effect of turning the white lead yellow; and nut oil should therefore be employed. If that is considered too expensive, one part of turpentine at least ought to be mixed with two parts of linseed oil.

Oil of Turpentine is more used than any of the preceding oils; the varnisher, indeed, scarcely employs any other. There is a great difference in the quality. The inferior kinds, though they may serve for mixing coarse and common colours, can never be used with good effect in varnish. The best description is that which is the lightest and least coloured. A simple method of trying its degree of goodness is with the best spirits of wine, which will take up about one-third part of the weight of the inferior sort of oil, and only about a seventh or eighth part of the best kinds.

Fat oils are often mixed with the oil of turpentine, as well as with other volatile oils—a mixture particularly hurtful in the case of varnishers. There is a remarkable distinction, however, between the two, by which such adulterations may be always readily detected. Both sorts of oil stain paper; but a stain from a volatile oil may be easily removed by heat, while one from fixed oils remains almost indelible. Thus if a drop of common oil be thrown on paper, and held near a fire, a part flies off; but before the whole of it can be dissipated, the paper is destroyed. If, on the contrary, a few drops of turpentine (or any other volatile oil) be thrown on paper and treated in the same way, the stain disappears without the texture of the paper being in the smallest degree injured. And if paper be stained with an oil compounded partly of a volatile and partly of a fat oil, that portion only which is volatile will evaporate on exposure to heat, while the other will remain.

It is owing to the property just mentioned that volatile oils are sometimes employed to make transparent paper for copying drawings.

For this purpose, the paper is besmeared with pure volatile oil of turpentine and dried for a short time, by exposure to air; it is then put on the drawing, the traces of which are distinctly seen through it. After taking off the copy by a pencil, the oil is easily expelled by holding the paper near the fire.

Drying Oils, which are composed of particular substances mixed with some of the oils before mentioned, are useful for several purposes. They are most valuable when so manufactured as to be colourless. They are much used in preparing varnishes; and, in oil painting, are not unfrequently employed as a varnish, either alone or diluted with a little oil of turpentine. Drying oil is easily procured at the shops; but, if you wish to make it yourself, one of the best methods is to take a pound of nut or linseed oil (according as it is intended for inside or outside work), to which a drying quality has been given by the method before mentioned; dissolve in it five ounces of rosin by means of a gentle heat; when this is done, add to it rather more than half an ounce of turpentine: let the composition rest till a sediment is formed and is quite cool; then pour it, free from any part of the sediment, into proper vessels, and make use of it while fresh. If at any time it should become too thick, you may dilute it with a little oil of turpentine.

Some painters of ornaments, and coach painters, instead of using drying oils, content themselves with adding white vitriol in mixing their colours. This method is bad; the salt of the vitriol will not unite with the oil, and the painting in consequence becomes mealy, and sometimes cracks.

When drying, oil is colourless; it is of great use to painters of pictures, by whom, as well as by the house painter, it is not unfrequently used as varnish, either in a pure or dilute state.

It has been recently discovered that when a solution of yellow soap is added to red, yellow, and black paints, when ground in oil, before they are casked up they acquire no improper hardness, and dry remarkably fast when laid on with the brush, without having recourse to any of the usual drying expedients.

Pilchard Oil, which possesses more greasy matter than any other fish oil, has been used in Cornwall for the last fifty years, to great advantage, in coarse painting. The preparation is said by a correspondent in the *Mechanics' Magazine* (vol. vi. page 471), to be made in the following manner: Put the oil into a clean iron pot, and place it over a slow fire (wood is best), to prevent it from burning; when it begins to heat, skim it well; let it remain on the fire till it singes a feather put therein. For every gallon of oil add a small tablespoonful of red litharge. Stir them together well for about three minutes; then take the pot off the fire, and let the mixture cool in the open air; after which it is fit for use. It is said to dry quickly, to incorporate well with any coloured paint on wood or iron, to have all the appearance of varnish, and to be extremely durable.

VARNISHES.

Strictly speaking, every substance, whether dry or liquid, is a varnish, which, being spread over any body, has the effect of giving its surface a brilliant appearance. But, in its general meaning, the term is only applied to those substances that are capable of rendering this effect *durable*.

The foundation of all varnishes are gummy and resinous substances; and the only liquids that can be combined with them, so as to form varnishes, are oils and spirit of wine.

For a varnish to be really good, it ought to be limpid, brilliant, transparent, and durable. The durability of a varnish is its greatest and rarest excellence.

The principal gums and resins used for varnishes are gum Arabic, gum elastic, gum anima, copal, dragon's blood, stick-lac, shell-lac, and mastic. The solvents chiefly employed are spirits of wine and spirits of turpentine.

In choosing gums and resins, those are to be preferred

which are quite free from particles of dirt, and of which the lumps, when held up to the light, present a clear and transparent appearance.

What is often sold at the shops as gum Arabic—the best of all the gums—is frequently only the clearer pieces of the gum Senegal, which, though equally strong and substantial, is far from being so pure as gum Arabic. The imposition may be detected by observing one very obvious distinction. The genuine gum Arabic is always in *small* irregular masses, *smooth on the outside;* the pieces of the gum Senegal are invariably larger, and *rough* on the outside.

A composition of different resins, coloured with brick-dust or Brazil-wood, or a very small portion of real dragon's blood, is not unfrequently sold as genuine. It is of a dull red or brick colour, whereas real dragon's blood is a dark red, and almost brown colour on the outside. The latter, too, is inflammable; while the imitation, when put into the fire, does not inflame, but swells up.

The liquid commonly sold under the name of *spirits of wine* is in general a highly rectified spirit, intermediate between proof spirit and alcohol, but not sufficiently concentrated for the purpose of making varnish. The readiest practicable method of determining whether the alcohol will answer your purpose is to fill a large phial with it, and then to drop into it a small lump of potash or pearlash which has been heated very hot over the fire, to expel its moisture, and not afterwards suffered to become cold: the phial is then to be well shaken; and if the lump remain dry, or nearly so, the alcohol is good; if any considerable portion of it remain undissolved, it is unfit for use.

Spirits of turpentine are always good in proportion to their inflammability—that which burns most readily being the best. The smell, too, of the inferior kind is more unpleasant and less powerful than that of the better sort.

When doubts are entertained as to its purity, pour about two tablespoonfuls into a saucer, and place it to evaporate in the sun, which it ought to do entirely in the course of two or three hours; if a greasy residuum or a soft sticky mucus is left, it is a proof that the turpentine is adulterated, and ought to be rejected.

Another method of judging of the comparative goodness of different sorts both of spirits of wine and spirits of turpentine, is by weighing quantities of two kinds equal in measure one against the other: *the lightest is always the best.*

The number of different varnishes to be obtained by various methods of mixing together the substances from which they can be manufactured is endless, and it would be altogether from the purpose and nature of this little work to attempt anything like a description of them. Many of them, indeed, are only useful to the artist, and are therefore not entitled to a place here while others are merely proofs of the ingenuity of chemical students, and from the expense or sacrifice of time attending their preparation, are not adapted for practical purposes. Almost every varnisher, too, has at least one or two compositions peculiar to himself, the superior value of which rests chiefly in his own opinion. In large towns and cities, moreover, the varnishes in common use can easily be purchased ready made; but for the benefit of those who may not have this convenience, or who prefer preparing their own varnishes, I shall here add a few simple recipes, from modern and approved sources, for making those that are in the most general use.

Shell-lac Varnish.

The best of the common spirit varnishes is that made with *shell-lac.* Hitherto the use of it has been limited in consequence of its possessing a brown yellowish colour, which made it unfit for all articles which that tint would injure; but Professor Hare, of Philadelphia, has made the arts a valuable present of the following method of producing it perfectly colourless: Dissolve in an iron kettle one part of pearlash in about eight parts of water; add one part of shell-lac, and heat the whole to ebullition. When the lac is dissolved, cool the solution and impregnate it with chlorine till the lac is all precipitated. The precipitate, is white, but its colour deepens by washing and consolidation; dissolved in alcohol, lac bleached by the above process yields a varnish which is as free from colour as any copal varnish. *Chlorine* (oxy-muriatic acid) may be formed by mixing intimately eight parts of common salt and three of the black oxide of manganese in powder: put this mixture into a retort; then pour four parts of sulphuric acid diluted with an equal weight of water and afterwards allowed to cool, upon the salt and manganese; the gas will then be immediately liberated, and the operation may be quickened by a moderate heat. A tube leading from the mouth of the retort must be passed into the resinous solution, when the gas will be absorbed and the lac precipitated.

It is to be presumed that, now that shell-lac varnish is thus rendered universally applicable, it will be the most used of any; as it possesses all the properties of a good spirit varnish in a higher degree than any of the other resins, and costs at the same time much less.

Shell-lac Varnish of various colours may be made by using any colour in fine powder with the varnish, in the following manner: Rub up the colour with a little alcohol, or spirits of turpentine, till it becomes perfectly smooth; then put it into the cup with the varnish.

Red Shell-lac Varnish

Is best made from good Dutch sealing-wax (which is itself chiefly composed of seed lac). This is the lac used to varnish glass or wood for electrical purposes. Three or four coats will make a perfect covering.

Turpentine Varnish.

Take five pounds of good clear rosin, pound it well, and put it into a gallon of oil of turpentine; boil the mixture over a stove, till the rosin is perfectly dissolved; and when cool, it will be fit for use.

Linseed Oil Varnish.

Boil any quantity of linseed oil for an hour, and to every pound of oil add four ounces of good clear rosin well powdered; keep stirring it till the rosin is perfectly dissolved, and when this is done, add one ounce of spirits of turpentine for every pound of oil, and when strained and cool it will be fit for use.

This varnish is much used for common purposes. It is cheap, is a good preservative of wood, and not liable to sustain injury from the application of hot water.

Copal Varnish.

Take one ounce of copal and half an ounce of shell-lac; powder them well, and put them into a bottle or jar containing a quart of spirits of wine. Place the mixture in a warm place, and shake it occasionally till you perceive that the gums are completely dissolved; and when strained, the varnish will be fit for use.

I have given the above as the simplest and therefore the most usual method of making common copal varnish; but it may be prepared in a variety of ways, where particular uses are required.

Gold-coloured Copal Varnish.

Take one ounce of powdered copal, two ounces of essential oil of lavender, and six ounces of essence of turpentine. Put the oil of lavender into a matras of a proper size, placed on a sand-bath subjected to a moderate heat. When the oil is very warm, add the copal from time to time, in very small quantities, and stir the mixture with a stick of white wood, rounded at the end. When the copal has entirely disappeared, put in the turpentine in almost a boiling state, at three different times, and keep continually stirring the mixture till the solution is quite completed.

When this varnish is required to be colourless, as is frequently the case, it will be necessary to use the rectified spirit of turpentine—the common essence sold at the shops being generally high coloured.

Camphorated Copal Varnish.

Take copal in powder, four ounces; essential oil of lavender, twelve ounces; camphor, a quarter of an ounce, and as much spirit of turpentine as will give the varnish the consistency required. Heat the oil and the camphor in a small matras, stirring them, and putting in the copal and turpentine in the manner directed in the preceding varnish.

This varnish is particularly well adapted for articles which require transparency and pliability, united to great durability, such as the varnished wire-gauze used in ships instead of glass.

Copal Varnish in Imitation of Tortoise-Shell.

Take of amber-coloured copal, six ounces; of shell-lac or Venice turpentine, an ounce and a half; twenty-four ounces of clear linseed oil, and six ounces of essence of turpentine. Place the copal in a matras and expose it to a moderate heat till it is liquefied; then add the linseed oil in a boiling state, afterwards the shell-lac or Venice turpentine, also liquefied, and lastly the spirit of turpentine in small portions. If the varnish prove too thick, dilute it with spirit of turpentine.

This varnish is principally used for watch-cases, though it is also applied to other imitations of tortoise-shell.

All the above methods, however, of preparing copal, require long boiling and careful filtering in the preparation, and consequently are not so convenient as the process first mentioned: they are therefore seldom used, unless where the nature of the substance to be varnished renders oil of turpentine decidedly preferable to spirits of wine.

An excellent copal varnish may be made by putting an ounce of copal of an amber colour, finely powdered, into a flask containing four ounces of ether; corking the mixture with a glass stopper, and shaking it for half an hour; then allowing it to rest till the liquor becomes perfectly clear.

It is unfortunate that the great volatility of ether and its very high price do not allow the use of this varnish for common purposes. Indeed, its employment is almost confined to repairing accidents in enamel, and restoring the smooth surface of paintings that have been cracked or shattered. It has some admirable properties which belong to no other varnish in existence. It presents great resistance to the friction of hard bodies, possesses remarkable solidity, has a peculiar drying quality, and a very fragrant smell.

Copal, and other varnishes, prepared with essence of turpentine, will not admit of being applied to purely white grounds, unless the turpentine has been highly rectified; and even then it is not unattended with risk. For coloured grounds, which require solidity, they are excellent.

The varnishes prepared with copal are some of the most useful and valuable known, and their composition has been much improved of late years. They are rich, splendid, and solid, bear friction well, and are of great service in preserving articles exposed to damp or rain. Mathematical and philosophical instruments are generally varnished with them.

Amber Varnish.

Put eight ounces of amber, finely powdered, into a vessel containing half a pint of the best spirits of turpentine (if for very fine purposes, rectified spirits of turpentine should be used); place the vessel over a stove or fire till the amber is quite melted; then put into it two ounces of shell-lac powdered, and place it on the fire again; keep stirring it till the gum is completely dissolved, and then add to the whole an ounce of clear cold-drawn linseed oil. Stir it well together, and when strained it will be fit for use.

Like copal varnish, this varnish may likewise be prepared in various ways; but the one here given is the cheapest and readiest, and the other methods of making it do not in any case possess advantages over this. Some varnishers prefer using more spirits of turpentine and a smaller proportion of linseed oil.

Some years since, amber varnish was in very general use; but of late, copal, on account of its being less coloured, has obtained a preference.

Caoutchouc, or Gum-Elastic Varnish.

Take eight ounces of gum-elastic, pound it well, and put it upon the fire in a vessel containing half a pound of boiling linseed oil. When the gum is dissolved, add half a pound of spirits of turpentine. Let them continue boiling together till the mixture becomes clear; and when it is cool, strain it for use.

This varnish is brilliant and durable; but it has the fault of drying very slowly, for which reason it is not employed.

Mastic Varnish.

This varnish, which is used principally for pictures in oil, is usually prepared by dissolving the mastic in spirits of turpentine by means of a sand-bath, then straining it through a fine sieve, and afterwards placing it, for two or three weeks, in a bottle well corked, where the light of the sun may act freely upon it, which causes a large precipitation of mucilaginous matter, and leaves the varnish as clear as water. But to procure a mastic varnish that can be perfectly depended upon, the following observations must be attended to: Let all the mastic be bruised by a muller on a grinding-stone; this will separate the soft or oily tears, as they are called, and enable you to throw them aside: whereas if the mastic is put in a mass into the turpentine, the tears remain embodied with it, and prevent the varnish from drying hard, leaving a greasy or tacky surface. The next point of importance is to make use only of turpentine which has been twice distilled, or which is at all events quite clear and colourless: you must take care not to have it served to you through an oily measure (as is too often the case), but poured out of the carboy without being shaken or disturbed. When the mastic and turpentine are thus obtained perfectly pure, they may be dissolved in a clean bottle *without heat, and by half an hour's shaking in the hand.* Let them then be strained and treated in the usual way, as above mentioned.

A varnish similar to this is occasionally made, in which frankincense or sandrac is employed instead of mastic, and is very well adapted for mixing up colours.

The French sometimes prepare this resin in pure alcohol; but mastic varnish thus prepared is liable to chill on the picture, and produces in time a kind of white scale over it, which injures its lustre.

Varnish for Violins, &c.

Take a gallon of rectified spirits of wine, twelve ounces of mastic, and a pint of turpentine varnish; put them all together in a tin can, and keep it in a very warm place, shaking it occasionally till it is perfectly dissolved; then strain it, and it is fit for use. If you find it necessary, you may dilute it with turpentine varnish.

This varnish is also very useful for furniture of plumtree, mahogany, or rosewood.

White hard Varnish.

Take one pound of mastic, four ounces of gum anima, and five pounds of gum sandrac: put them altogether, to dissolve, into a vessel containing two ounces of rectified spirits of wine, which should be kept in a warm place and frequently shaken till all the gums are quite dissolved; then strain the mixture through a lawn sieve, and it will be fit for use.

Varnishes for Paling and coarse Wood-work.

Grind any quantity of tar with as much Spanish brown as it will bear without becoming too thick to be used as a paint or varnish; then spread it on the wood with a large brush. It soon hardens by keeping. The work should be kept as free from dust and insects as possible, till the varnish is thoroughly dry.

This varnish is an excellent preserver of the wood from damp; on which account, as well as its being cheaper, it is to be preferred to painting, not only for paling, but for weather-boarding, and all coarser kinds of painting on wood.

The colour may be made a grayish instead of a glossy brown, by mixing a small proportion of white lead, or of whiting and ivory black, with the Spanish brown.

Varnish for Coloured Drawings.

Mix together one ounce of Canada balsam and two ounces of spirits of turpentine. Before applying the composition, size the drawing or print with a solution of isinglass in water; when this is dry, apply the varnish with a camel's-hair brush.

The use of this varnish gives to coloured drawings and prints an appearance resembling that of oil paintings.

Varnish for Glass.

Reduce a quantity of gum tragacanth to powder, and let it dissolve for twenty-four hours in the white of eggs well beat up; then rub it gently on the glass with a brush.

Black Varnish for old Straw or Chip Hats.

Take half an ounce of the best black sealing-wax, pound it well, and put it into a four-ounce phial containing two ounces of rectified spirits of wine. Place it in a sand-bath, or near a moderate fire, till the wax is dissolved; then lay it on warm, with a fine soft hair brush, before a fire or in the sun. It gives a good stiffness to old straw hats, and a beautiful gloss equal to new. It likewise resists wet.

Varnish for Drawings and Card Work.

Boil some clean parchment-cuttings in water, in a glazed pipkin, till they produce a very clear size. Strain it, and keep it for use.

Changing Varnishes.

Varnishes of this description are called changing, because, when applied to metals, such as copper, brass, or hammered tin, they give them a more agreeable colour. Indeed, the common metals, when coated with them, acquire a lustre approaching to that of the precious metals, and hence these varnishes are much employed in manufacturing imitations of gold and silver.

It would be an endless task to enumerate all the various kinds of changing varnishes that can be made and the methods of preparing them. One simple mode of mixing I shall, however, mention here, by which all the different tints that can be required for changing varnishes may be certainly obtained.

Put four ounces of the best gum gamboge into thirty-two ounces of spirits of turpentine; four ounces of dragon's blood into the same quantity of spirits of turpentine as the gamboge; and one ounce of anatto into eight ounces of the same spirits. The three mixtures should be made in different vessels.

They should then be kept for about a fortnight, in a warm place, and as much exposed to the sun as possible.

At the end of that time they will be fit for use; and you can procure any tints you wish by making a composition from them with such proportions of each liquor as practice and the nature of the colour you are desirous of obtaining will point out.

Changing varnishes may likewise be employed, with very good effect, for furniture.—*See Lacquers.*

Mordant Varnishes.

These are a species of varnishes chiefly employed when a coating of some other substance is to be entirely or in part laid over them.

Compositions of this kind ought neither to be too thick nor too fluid, as either of these faults injures the delicacy of the gilding.

They should likewise be of rather a fat nature, because they must be so prepared as not to dry till the gilding is completed.

Various compositions are employed as mordants, and almost every workman has a favourite one of his own. One of the best is the following:—

Dissolve one ounce of mastic, one ounce of sandrac, half an ounce of gum gamboge, and a quarter of an ounce of turpentine in six ounces of spirits of turpentine.

Another good mordant may be obtained by exposing boiled oil to a strong heat in a pan, and, when you perceive a black smoke disengaged from it, setting it on fire and extinguishing it in a few moments by putting on the cover of the pan. Then pour the matter while it is warm into a heated bottle, and add to it a little oil of turpentine.

Both the above mordants have something of a drying nature, and are therefore objectionable when the work to be done, after the application of the mordant, is of a kind that requires it to be a long time before drying. In such cases, the best mordant is formed by adding a little red lead to the copal varnish prepared with camphor and oil of lavender, as before directed.

The choice of mordants must in some measure be guided by the tone which you desire to give to your work, whether deep or light, red or yellow. For bronzing or very pale gilding, a mixture of asphaltum and drying oil, diluted with oil of turpentine, is much recommended.

One of the simplest mordants is that procured by dissolving a little honey in thick glue. It has the effect of greatly heightening the colour of the gold, and the leaf sticks to it extremely well.

GENERAL OBSERVATIONS ON VARNISHES.

It is a common practice in the manufacture of spirit varnishes to mix glass or sand with the gum or resin, for the purpose of enabling the alcohol to penetrate more readily into all parts of the mass. M. Ferrari, however, recommends (*Giornale de Fissica*, ix. p. 36) that in place of those substances a coarsely-powdered charcoal should be used; for the glass or sand generally tends to aggregate the gum or resin at the bottom of the vessels and to protect it from the solvent; whilst, on the contrary, the charcoal rather tends to raise and divide it. The most advantageous proportion appears to be one ounce of charcoal to one pound of the spirit or the oil of turpentine used. The uses to which different varnishes are to be applied must, of course, determine the choice of them. Good varnishes, prepared with spirits of wine, are very clear, brilliant, and delicate, and may be applied with success to furniture, and to fancy ornaments which are kept within doors, and admit of re-varnishing easily; but they have not body nor durability enough for coloured grounds—not even wainscoting, ceiling ornaments, &c., or any articles exposed to the weather. If you attempt to renovate them by rubbing, they become of a mealy appearance. Their inferiority to oil varnishes is evident from the circumstance that oils will of themselves form varnishes by repeated application, whereas spirits of wine alone, so applied, disappear without leaving any trace.

Varnishes made with turpentine or other oils are much superior in many respects to those prepared with spirits of wine. They are pliable and smooth, as well as brilliant and durable. They yield better to the operation of polishing, and are less liable to crack.

Oil of poppies, nut oil, and linseed oil are used for making fat varnishes; oil of turpentine and oil of lavender for the drier ones. The other oils are either too fat, too much coloured, or too dear, to answer the purpose of the varnisher.

Oil of turpentine might be employed on all occasions instead of spirits of wine, in the composition of varnishes were it not for the strong and disagreeable smell arising from it. The oil obtained from the coarse or common turpentine ought never to be used in the preparation of varnishes. A slight coating of spirits of wine varnish laid over one coat of turpentine, when dry, is of great use in removing the offensive odour.

Varnishes are usually kept in large strong glass bottles with a wide mouth, for the convenience of taking them out; but as the light is frequently found to act strongly upon them, and render them thick, I would recommend wrapping up the bottles in sheep-skin, or moist parchment, folding it round the neck, and tying it with several turns of pack-thread.

The best vessel for holding your varnish while using it, is a varnish-pan, which may be had at any colour-shop. It is made of tin, with a false bottom; the interval between the two bottoms is filled with sand, which, being heated over the fire, keeps the varnish fluid, and makes it flow more readily from the brush. There is a tin handle to the pan, and the false bottom comes sloping from one end to the other which causes the varnish to run to one end.

Very great caution is required in the making of varnish—a process in which most serious accidents have frequently occurred.

As heat in many cases is necessary to dissolve the gums used in making varnish, the best way, when practicable, is to use what the chemists call a sand-bath, which is simply placing the vessel in which the varnish is in another filled with sand and placed on the fire; this will generally be sufficient to prevent the spirits catching fire; but in case of such accidents (which not unfrequently happen), it will be best to take a vessel so large that there shall be little danger of spilling any—indeed, the vessel should never be more than two-thirds filled; but in case of accidents, have ready at hand a piece of board sufficiently large to cover the top of the vessel in case of its taking fire, as also a wet wrapper, in case it should be spilt when on the fire, as water by itself thrown on it only increases the mischief. The person who attends the varnish-pot should also have his hands covered with gloves, and if these are made of leather, and rather damp, it will effectually prevent injury.

POLISHES.

The compositions used for polishing are different, according to the nature of the varnish for which they are employed. Some of the most useful I shall insert here.

Varnish Polish.

Take two ounces of tripoli, reduced to fine powder; put it into an earthen pot or basin, with water to cover it; then take a piece of fine flannel four times doubled, lay it over a piece of cork or rubber, and proceed to polish your varnish, always wetting it with the tripoli and water. You will know when the process is completed by wiping a part of the work with a sponge and observing whether there is a fair and even gloss. Take a bit of mutton suet and fine flour, and clean off the work.

Or, the powdered tripoli may be mixed up with a little pure oil and used upon a ball of serge, or of chamois leather, which is better. The polishing may afterwards be completed with a bit of serge or cloth, without tripoli.

Putty powder, and even common whiting and water, are sometimes used for polishing; but they produce a very inferior effect to tripoli, except in the case of ivory, for which putty and water, used upon a rubber made of a hat, forms the best and quickest polish.

Putty and water may likewise be used, in the same manner as just mentioned for ivory, in finishing off the polish of pearl-work, after it has first been polished very smooth with pumice-stone, finely powdered, and well washed to free it from impurities and dirt.

Polish for Dark-coloured Woods.

Take one ounce of seed-lac, two drachms of gum-guaiacum, two drachms of dragon's blood, and two drachms of gum mastic: put them into a vessel containing a pint of spirit of wine: stop the vessel close, and expose the mixture to a moderate heat till you find all the gums dissolved: strain it off into a bottle for use, with a quarter of a gill of linseed oil, to be shaken up well with it.

The dragon's blood, which is apt to give a red tinge, renders this polish improper for light-coloured woods.

Polish for Tunbridge Ware Goods, &c.

Take half an ounce of gum sandrac and two ounces of gum benjamin; put them into a glass bottle, with a pint of spirits of wine. Cork the bottle, and place it in a sand-bath, or in hot water, till you find the gums dissolved, shaking it in the interim from time to time. When it is all dissolved, strain it through a muslin sieve, and bottle it for use.

Carver's Polish.

In a pint of spirits of wine, dissolve two ounces of seed-lac and two ounces of white rosin.

The principal use of this polish is for the carved parts of cabinet-work, such as standards, pillars, claws, &c. It should be laid on warm; and if the work can also be warmed at the time, it will be still better; but all moisture and dampness should be carefully avoided.

French Polish.

Take one ounce of shell-lac, a quarter of an ounce of gum Arabic, and a quarter of an ounce of gum copal. Bruise them well, and sift them through a piece of muslin: then put them, along with a pint of spirits of wine, into a closely-corked vessel: place it in a very warm situation, and shake it frequently every day till the gums are dissolved: then strain it through a piece of muslin, and keep it tight corked for use.

Water-proof Polish.

Put two ounces of gum benjamin, a quarter of an ounce of gum sandrac, and a quarter of an ounce of gum anima, into a pint of spirits of wine, in a closely-stopped bottle. Place the bottle either in a sand-bath or in hot water, till the gums are dissolved; then strain off the mixture, shake it up with a quarter of a gill of the best clear poppy oil, and put it by for use.

Finishing Polish.

Put two drachms of shell-lac and two drachms of gum-benjamin into half a pint of the very best rectified spirits of wine, in a bottle closely corked. Keep the bottle in a warm place, and shake it frequently till the gums are dissolved; when cold, shake up with it two teaspoonfuls of the best clear poppy oil, and it will be fit for use.

This polish may be applied with great advantage after any of those mentioned in the foregoing recipes have been used. It removes the defects existing in them, increases their lustre and durability, and gives the surface a most brilliant appearance.

GILDING MATERIALS.

True Gold Powder.

PUT some gold leaf, with a little honey or thick gum-water, into an earthen mortar, and pound the mixture till the gold is reduced to very small particles. Then wash out the honey or gum repeatedly with warm water, and the gold will be left behind in the state of powder; which, when dried, is fit for use.

Another, and perhaps better method of preparing gold powder, is to heat a prepared amalgam* of gold in a clean open crucible, continuing a very strong heat till all the mercury has evaporated, stirring the amalgam all the while with a glass rod. When the mercury has entirely left the gold, grind the remainder in a Wedgewood's mortar, with a little water; and when dried, it will be fit for use. The subliming the mercury is, however, a process injurious to the health.

Colour-Heightening Compositions.

For Yellow Gold, dissolve in water six ounces of saltpetre, two ounces of copperas, one ounce of white vitriol,

---

* An amalgam of any metal is formed by a mixture of quicksilver with that metal.

and one ounce of alum. If wanted redder, add a small portion of blue vitriol.

For Green Gold, dissolve in water a mixture consisting of an ounce and a half of saltpetre, vitriol, and sal ammoniac an ounce and a quarter each, and one ounce of verdigris.

For Red Gold, take an ounce and a half of red ochre in fine powder, the same quantity of *calcined* verdigris, half an ounce of calcined borax, and four ounces of melted yellow wax. The verdigris must be calcined; or else, by the heat applied in melting the wax, the vinegar becomes so concentrated as to corrode the surface, and make it appear speckled.

Mosaic Gold.

Mosaic Gold, or *Aurum Mosaicum*, is used for inferior articles. It is prepared in the following manner: A pound of tin is melted in a crucible, and half a pound of purified quicksilver added to it: when this mixture is cold, it is reduced to powder, and ground with half a pound of sal ammoniac and seven ounces of flower of sulphur, till the whole is thoroughly mixed. They are then calcined in a matras; and the sublimation of the other ingredients leaves the tin converted into the *aurum Mosaicum*, which is found at the bottom of the glass, like a mass of bright flaky gold powder. Should any black or discoloured particles appear, they must be removed. The sal ammoniac used here must be very white and clear, and the mercury quite pure and unadulterated. When a shade of deeper red is required, it can easily be obtained by grinding a very small quantity of red lead along with the above materials.

Dutch or German Gold.

A gilding powder is sometimes made from Dutch Gold, which is sold in books at a very low price. This is treated in the same way as the real gold leaf in making the true gold powder. It is necessary, when this inferior powder is used, to cover the gilding with a coat of clear varnish; otherwise it soon loses its metallic appearance. The same remark applies, though in a less degree, to Mosaic gilding.

Ethereal Solution of Gold.

The following mode of effecting this solution (used chiefly for gilding steel) is recommended by Mr. H. Mill, in the "Technical Repository," as being superior to any previously made known. "The instructions," he says, "given in most elementary works on chemistry for this purpose are either erroneous or not sufficiently explicit." The process answers equally well for either gold or platina.

Dissolve any quantity of gold or platina in nitro-muriatic acid (*aqua regia*), until no further effervescence is occasioned by the application of heat. Evaporate the solution of gold or platina, thus formed, to dryness, in a gentle heat (it will then be freed from all excess of acid, which is essential), and re-dissolve the dry mass in as little water as possible: next take an instrument which is used by chemists for dropping liquids, known by the name of a separating funnel, having a pear-shaped body, tapering to a fine sharp point, and a neck capable of being stopped with the finger or a cork, which may contain a liquid ounce or more; fill it with the liquid about one-quarter part, and the other three parts must be filled with the very best sulphuric ether. If this be rightly managed, the two liquids will not mix. Then place the tube in a horizontal position, and gently turn it round with the finger and thumb. The ether will very soon be impregnated with the gold or platina, which may be known by its changing its colour: replace it in a perpendicular position, and let it rest for twenty-four hours; having first stopped up the upper orifice with a cork. The liquid will then be divided into two parts—the darkest colouring being underneath. To separate them, take out the cork and let the dark liquid flow out: when it has disappeared, stop the tube immediately with the cork, and what remains in the tube is fit for use, and may be called gilding liquid. Let it be put into a bottle and tightly corked.

The muriate of gold or platina, formed by digesting these metals in nitro-muriatic acid, must be entirely free from all excess of acid; because it will otherwise act too forcibly on the steel, and cause the coating of gold to peel off. Pure gold must be employed: the ether must not be shaken with the muriate of gold, as is advised in chemical publications, for it will be sure, then, to contain acid; but if the two liquids be brought continually into contact by the motion described, the affinity between ether and gold is so strong as to overcome the obstacle of gravity, and it will hold the gold in solution. The ethereal solution may also be concentrated by gentle evaporation.

Gold Oil Colour, or Size.

The English method of preparing the colour in size which serves as the ground on which the gold is laid, is to grind together some red oxide of lead with the thickest drying oil that can be procured—the older the better. To make it work freely, it is mixed before being used with a little oil of turpentine, till it is brought to a proper consistence. (See also *Mordant Varnishes.*)

Gold Water Size.

One pound of Armenian bole, two ounces of red lead, and a sufficient portion of black lead, are ground separately in water, and then mixed, and re-ground with nearly a spoonful of olive oil. The gold size is tempered by mixing it in parchment size which is clear and clean, and has been passed through a fine sieve to clear it of all foreign matters. The *parchment* size is made by boiling down pieces of white leather, or clippings of parchment, till they are reduced to a stiff jelly.

Preparatory Size.

Boil a handful of the leaves of wormwood and two or three heads of garlic in a quart of water, until the liquid is reduced to one-half; then strain it through a cloth, and add half a handful of common salt, and nearly half a pint of vinegar. The design of this composition (usually employed in gilding looking-glass and picture frames) is to obviate the greasiness of the wood, and prepare it the better to receive the coats which are to be laid on, and to preserve it from the ravages of worms. When used, it is mixed with a sufficient portion of good glue, boiling hot. In applying it to the gilding of plaster or marble, the salt must be left out of its composition; as, in damp situations, this would produce a white saline efflorescence on the surface of the gold.

White Coating.

A quart of strong parchment size and half a pint of water are to be made quite hot, and to this are to be added (in small portions from time to time) two good handfuls of common whiting passed through a fine sieve; this mixture is to be left to infuse for half an hour, when it is to be stirred carefully so that the amalgamation may be perfect.

Colouring Yellow.

Half a pint of parchment size is taken, which must be clean, white, and clear, and of one-half the strength of that used for the white coating; this is warmed, and there is mixed with it two ounces of yellow ochre, very finely ground in water; it is then left at rest, and the clear portion decanted, which gives a fine yellow colour, that serves, in water gilding, to cover those deep recesses into which the gold cannot be made to enter: it serves also as a mordant for the gold size.

Vermeil.

This is a liquid which gives to the gold a warm reflection. It is composed of two ounces of anotto, one ounce of gamboge, one ounce of vermilion, half an ounce of dragon's blood, two ounces of salt of tartar, and eighteen grains of good saffron. The whole is to be boiled in a quart of water, over a slow fire, until it is reduced to one-fourth, when the liquor is passed through a strainer of silk or muslin.

MISCELLANEOUS MATERIALS.

Painter's Cream.

This is a preparation sometimes employed by painters when they are obliged to leave work unfinished for a length of time. They cover the parts already painted with it, which preserves the freshness of their colours, and can be easily removed when they return to their work. It is made as follows:—

Take half an ounce of the best mastic, finely powdered, and dissolve it over a gentle fire, in three ounces of very clear nut-oil. Pour the mixture into a marble mortar, with two drachms of pounded sugar of lead at the bottom of it. Stir this with a wooden pestle, and keep adding water in small quantities till the whole is of the appearance and thickness of cream, and refuses to admit more water, so as to mix freely.

Rotten Stone.

Rotten stone is sometimes harsh and gritty; the best way of trying it is to take a little between the teeth, when the least portion of grit may be detected. Careful workmen will always wash it before they use it. This is effected by stirring the fine powder in a considerable quantity of water, then allowing it to remain at rest for a few seconds, and pouring the water into a glazed earthen vessel; the powder which then precipitates will be perfectly fine and smooth; by washing the remainder, the whole of the finer parts may be separated from the grit.

Glue and Isinglass.

Good glue should swell when kept in cold water for three or four days: it should be semi-transparent, of a brown colour, and free from cloudiness. Before using it, it should be broken into small pieces, covered with cold water for some hours to soften it, then boiled till dissolved, and again allowed to congeal by cooling. The books in general recommend, as a size for gilding and bronzing, a solution of isinglass; but one of good clear common glue is much cheaper, and answers equally well. Isinglass, though a purer gelatine than glue, is not so easily dissolved.

Common Size.

The size used by painters for most sorts of common work is prepared by boiling in water pieces of parchment and of the skins of animals and fins of fish, and evaporating the solution to a proper consistency. It only differs, however, from a solution of glue in containing fewer foreign ingredients and in not being so strong.

GRINDING AND WASHING COLOURS.

The following directions for the grinding of colours will be found of use to those who may not find it convenient to have a mill for the purpose, such as that we have described in a former part of our work.

In grinding, place yourself in such a situation, with respect to the grinding-stone, that you may be able with ease to exercise the full length and strength of your arms in the use of the muller. Then place upon the stone a *small quantity* of the colour you are about to grind, not above two-thirds of a common saucer full at most. Novices are apt to entertain an idea that the work would be hastened by grinding a great deal at once, but this is a mistake. The less you grind at a time the easier will be the process and the finer the colour. One of the most essential points in the preparation of a colour is its being reduced into as small parts as possible. The beauty of its appearance and the profit arising from it equally depend upon this: and a good workman will not therefore grudge the time employed in the operation. When you have laid your colour on the stone, pour upon it a little of the oil or varnish with which you intend to grind it, being careful not to put too much at first. Mix the oil and the colour together; then place the muller upon them, and turn it a few times about. If you find there is not oil enough, add a little more, and continue to grind till the colour becomes of the consistence of an ointment. Be careful not to add too much oil so as to make the colour too thin and cause it to run about the stone; for then it will be necessary to add more solid matter, which would occasion a great waste of time and labour. When the colour is rendered thinner than it should be, the grinding is less fatiguing, but it occupies more time; when thicker, the work is more laborious, but more speedily executed. Experience will teach you to judge correctly in this matter.

Should the colour spread during the grinding, you must bring it together with your palette-knife or voider. When you have ground it sufficiently fine, which you may determine by the difficulty of raising the muller from the stone, and by the noise occasioned by the grinding at first almost entirely subsiding, take up the muller; then if you find the colour completely smooth like butter, without any grittiness, take it off the stone with a palette-knife or spatula, and put it into your pot or pan. Afterwards lay more colour upon the stone, and continue grinding in the same manner till the necessary quantity is ground.

It is always desirable to grind at one time as much of a colour as is required for the work you have in hand: if you prepare it at intervals, in different quantities, you will often find some difficulty in procuring exactly the same shade or tint; and if you fail in this, the appearance of the work will be sadly disfigured. Should any colour happen to be left which you are desirous of preserving, you have only to cover it with water and deposit it in a cool place. It is likewise advisable to take the same precaution with your colours, if you have occasion to rest for a time, as it will prevent their drying, even in the hottest weather.

It is not unusual with painters and varnishers, who have much business, to grind or prepare at once quantities of different colours or varnishes sufficient to serve them for a long while. These, as the best mode of preserving them, they keep tied up close in ox or sheep bladders, so as to be always ready when wanted.

Colours that are of a coarse and sandy nature can seldom be ground to a proper degree of fineness. Where common work only is required, this is not very material; but in cases where superior delicacy is necessary, such colours, after being ground, must undergo the operation of washing.

The chief of these are yellow ochre, charcoal, bone-black, Spanish brown, red lead, white chalk, verditer, and Saxon blue.

In washing colours, put the quantity you wish to clean into a vessel of clear water, and stir it till the water becomes coloured; skim off any filth you observe swimming at the top; and when you think the grossest part of the colour is settled at the bottom, pour off the water into a second vessel large enough to hold four or five times as much water as the first; then pour some more water into the first vessel, and proceed as before. Keep repeating this till you find all the fine part of the colour drawn off, and none but the gritty particles remaining in the bottom of the first vessel. Let the water in the larger vessel stand till it be quite clear and all the colour settled at the bottom; then pour the water off from it, and the colour at the bottom, *when completely dried*, will be fit for use.

Colours, whether you grind them yourself, as above directed, or purchase them ready ground, will, in that state, be too thick for use, and it will be necessary to dilute them with the varnish or oil you propose to employ in order to bring them to a proper consistence. In doing this, extremes must be carefully avoided. If the colour be made too thin, it runs, and does not cover the article to be painted equally or exactly; if too thick it forms lumps, is hard to spread, occasions more expense, disfigures the work, and fatigues the hand which applies it. If, when the brush is taken from the pot and turned two or three times round in the hand, being held obliquely so as to check the thread which is formed, the colour do not drop from it, it will then be as stiff as it can be well wrought with; and this is the proper state for use, as both expedition and durability are gained by it. If it be thin enough to allow the ground on which it is laid to be at all seen through it, it cannot be good; and though it may work more easily at the time, it will require repeated coatings to make it perfect and substantial, when one of a proper thickness would have been sufficient. I may here remark that many jobs being contracted for by painters at so much a yard, and the work to be coloured *three times over*, some are in the habit, with a view of sparing paint and labour, of making their colourings so thin as not to be altogether equal to one good coating. But this is a practice which no tradesman who values his own character or that of the work turned out of his hands will adopt.

CLEANLINESS IN WORKING.

The principal end aimed at by the Painter, Varnisher, or Gilder, and especially by the last two, is to beautify; and, without the strictest cleanliness, it is obvious this end can never be answered.

Every surface to which colour, varnish, or gilding is to be applied, should first be thoroughly cleaned; it should be rubbed, brushed, and even washed, if necessary; in the last case, however, it must be well dried afterwards.

When any surface which is to be varnished or painted has been previously varnished and is found to be encrusted with dust or dirt, soap and water must be applied gently with a sponge, and great care taken every time after the sponge has been rubbed over the varnish to rinse it in clean water, and to squeeze it thoroughly out before it be again dipped into the soap and water.

In grinding colours, after you have ground as much of any one sort as you want, before you proceed to place any other kind upon the stone, let it be perfectly cleaned from the former colour, by first rubbing it with a cloth and fine dry ashes or sand, and afterwards with a little spirit of turpentine; then let it be well wiped with a rag, or with leather shavings.

But of all things in which cleanliness is essential, brushes and pencils are, perhaps, the most to be considered. With regard to the painter, where the very greatest nicety is required, a separate brush or pencil should be assigned to each colour, wiped when the work is done, and preserved by covering it with water. With artists, this is an invariable rule, but the occupations of the mechanical painter are hardly ever of such extreme delicacy as to require him to adopt it. In general, it is sufficient for him to carefully wash out every brush or pencil, after he has done with it, or before he employs it for any other colour than that with which he has been previously using it. This washing out should be first in the oil with which the colour has been ground or mixed (but neat linseed oil, or oil of turpentine, will always sufficiently answer for general purposes), and afterwards in warm soap-suds. Brushes that have been used for varnishing may, on an emergency, be tolerably washed out with boiling water and yellow soap only. It is, however, much better to wash them well first with spirit of wine, if the varnish has been compounded with spirits; or with oil of turpentine, if it has been prepared with any description of oil; and, in either case, to clean them thoroughly with warm soap and water. The spirits used for washing varnish brushes are not thereby rendered unfit for use in preparing varnishes for common purposes. Remember, if either oil or colour be once allowed to dry in a brush or pencil, it is spoiled for ever. For coloured varnishes, kept in small quantities, a brush may be appropriated to each exclusively, and left in the bottle; but in this case the cork should be perforated so as to fit the handle, and the points of the hairs should dip into the varnish; the brush will then be always ready for use. A common mustard bottle will in general answer the purpose.

PRACTICE OF PAINTING.

A PAINTER will consult durability in preference to beauty of appearance, or the reverse, according as his work is to be more or less exposed to the weather. In out-door work, durability is of course of the most consequence; and as it is likewise the simplest kind of painting, I shall begin with noticing the manner of executing it.

Before attempting to lay any colour upon your work, you must carefully fill up with putty, so as to make the whole surface perfectly level, all flaws, cracks, openings, nail-holes, &c.; for if this be not done, the rain and snow will be sure to penetrate into these places and quickly destroy the fruits of your labour. All knots and unevennesses must likewise be carefully removed. When these points are accomplished, proceed to the *priming* of the work, that is, laying on the colour which is to serve as a ground for the succeeding coatings. The nature of the priming will, of course, be regulated by that which the surface is ultimately to receive. Sufficient time must be allowed for this to dry, according to the state of the weather: from two to three days will generally be enough. When the wood is new, or great solidity required in the work, it may be proper to repeat the first priming; otherwise, when that is dry, proceed to put on the first coat of your proposed colour, and afterwards the others in succession, as each of the preceding ones become dry. The number of coats applied will depend upon the agreement made, and upon how far the work is wanted to be finished and substantial.

When the wood you are about to colour is new, the priming should be laid on as thin as possible; because, in this case, the quantity of oil which necessarily sinks into the wood is very useful in preserving it. This thinness of the priming in new wood is also the reason why, as before observed, it is proper to repeat it. But as the thinness tends to delay its drying, if the priming colour be one that is naturally hard to dry, do not mix it with plain linseed oil, but with one part of drying oil and two parts of linseed oil; or if the priming colour be white or blue, mix it with linseed oil as usual, but grind a small portion of white copperas along with it, because the two colours just mentioned are affected in their tints by the drying oil.

No new coating of colour ought ever to be applied till the former is perfectly dry, which can never be the case while the least stickiness is felt on applying the hand to it. The neglect of this precaution is certain to ruin all the beauty of painting. Great care should likewise be taken to brush off any dust which may have settled upon the former coat before applying a new one; for, if it be allowed to remain and mix with the colour, the uniformity of the tint will be destroyed, particularly in bright colours. The workmen ought to be very careful that every coating is of the same thickness throughout, or the work when done will have an unfinished and slovenly appearance. This forms an additional reason for always mixing as much colour at once as is necessary for the job to which it is to be applied. The proper thickness of each respective coating can only be learned by habit and experience. If too thin, it often cracks in drying; if too thick it becomes blistered, wrinkled, and unequal. The first coating, however, may always allowably be made much thinner than any of the succeeding ones.

Practice, too, is necessary, in order to obtain even the proper use of the brush, and to learn the art of varying its strokes according to circumstances. Sometimes long strokes are to be employed to extend the colour in a uniform manner; at other times the colour should be laid on in repeated dabs, for the purpose of encrusting it in recesses and places where the surface is unequal. The test of the complete workman in this respect is to leave no marks of the brush behind him.

The same general directions that are given for outside painting will apply to inside work; but in this latter, more finish and delicacy of execution are necessary than in the former; and as it is not so much exposed to injury from the effects of weather and the state of the atmosphere as the work done without-doors, the painter is not obliged to pay so much attention to durability, but, in the choice and application of his colours, principally to regard beauty and effect. In inside work, the surfaces to be painted are frequently composed of fir or deal, in which kinds of wood, particularly when new, there are usually a great many resinous knots. If these be permitted to remain, the colour will run into them and not adhere. Before beginning to paint, you should, therefore, saturate these knots with a mixture of red lead and litharge with a small quantity of oil of turpentine.

The paneling of wainscot, and other similar parts of inside work, will give you frequent occasion to employ very small brushes or pencils. In using these, you should not take your colours out of a pot or pan, but have those that you want disposed upon a palette. There is more than one advantage attached to this. In the first place, if your pencil be only dipped into a pot of colour, it brings out with it no more than hangs on the outside—a quantity, from the small size of the brush, that will go but a little way in working; whereas, if you work and temper the colour by rubbing the pencil about in it upon the palette, it will imbibe a considerable quantity of the colour. In addition to this, you will likewise, by this method, be able to work your pencil to a point, which is a great advantage in fine painting and drawing lines, and which you could never obtain by taking your colour upon it out of a pot.

Painting in Distemper.

The leading difference between oil-painting and painting in distemper is, that in the latter the colours, instead of being prepared with oil, are mixed with size and water. This circumstance renders many colouring substances, particularly some that contain chalk or clayey earth, or are extracted from vegetable matter, proper for the purpose of distemper, which cannot be used in painting in oil.

Almost all colouring substances which can be used in oil-painting are applicable in distemper; but the reverse, as will appear from the remarks I have just made, is far from being the case. In speaking of colours, care has been taken to notice particularly such as, from their nature, can be employed only in distemper.

In painting in distemper, it is advisable to apply all the coatings, except the last, warm; not, however, in a boiling state, for that is injurious, and may cause wood to split. Besides, if the size be too much heated, it becomes fat, and will not adhere. In putting on fresh coatings, be very careful to preserve an equal thickness throughout.

Without the utmost attention to having the ground you are to work upon perfectly clean, no pleasing effect can ever result from distemper. Grease and lime on the surface that is to receive it would ruin all. They must be removed by scraping if the surface be a wall, and by a solution of pearl-ash if it be wood. Canvas must be cleaned by means of a ley.

When the wall or surface is very smooth, a coating of warm glue is first applied; but if rough, a coat of Spanish white, or chalk mixed with a solution of glue, is employed to render the surface smoother; and when the coating is dry, it is scraped as clean and as even as possible. A level surface is indispensable to receive distemper. If there are any considerable inequalities or holes, they must be filled up with gypsum, and time allowed, before applying any coat, for that gypsum to gain body, which will not be the case before it is thoroughly dry.

In painting in distemper, the thickness of the colour, contrary to the observation I made on that head in oil-painting, should be such that it may run or drop from the brush in a thread when taken from the pot. If the colour do not form a thread, it is too thick, and the work is likely to become scaly.

Distemper is much used in the interior of houses, and when well executed has a very delicate and beautiful appearance. It is likewise free from the disagreeable smell which usually arises from the turpentine in oil-painting. It is, however, far inferior to oil, both as to the durability of the colours and to the preservation of the surfaces on which it is applied. In some cases, too, it is attended with the inconvenience of not enabling the workman to see what effect a particular mixture will produce when it is dry. When this happens, the only method of obviating the evil is to try each mixture on pieces of prepared wood having the same tint as the ground on which you are working, so as to obtain the real tint.

A kind of distemper, called by the French *badigeon*, is sometimes used in out-door work, to give a uniform tint to houses rendered brown by time, and to churches where it is required to render them brighter. It has generally a yellow tint. The best kind is made by mixing the saw-dust or powder of the same kind of stone and slaked lime, in a bucket of water containing a pound of alum in solution. The composition is applied with a brush.

Painting in Milk.

In consequence of the injury which has often resulted to sick and weakly persons from the smell of common paint, the following method of painting with milk has been adopted by some workmen, which, for the interior of buildings, besides being as free as distemper from any offensive odour, is said to be nearly equal to oil-painting in body and durability.

Take half a gallon of skimmed milk, six ounces of lime newly slaked,* four ounces of poppy, linseed, or nut-oil, and three pounds of Spanish white. Put the lime into an earthen vessel or clean bucket, and having poured on it a sufficient quantity of milk to make it about the thickness of cream, add the oil in small quantities at a time, stirring the mixture with a wooden spatula. Then put in the rest of the milk, and afterwards the Spanish white.

It is, in general, indifferent which of the oils abovementioned you use; but, for a pure white, oil of poppy is the best.

The oil in this composition, being dissolved by the

---

* Lime is slaked by dipping it into water, then taking the pieces out immediately and allowing them to slake in the open air.

lime, wholly disappears; and, uniting with the whole of the other ingredients, forms a kind of calcareous soap.

In putting in the Spanish white, you must be careful that it is finely powdered and strewed gently over the surface of the mixture. It then, by degrees, imbibes the liquid and sinks to the bottom.

Milk skimmed in summer is often found to be curdled; but this is of no consequence in the present preparation, as its combining with the lime soon restores it to its fluid state. But it must on no account be sour; because, in that case, it would, by uniting with the lime, form an earthy salt, which could not resist any degree of dampness in the air.

Milk paint may likewise be used for out-door objects by adding to the ingredients before-mentioned two ounces each more of oil and slaked lime, and two ounces of Burgundy pitch. The pitch should be put into the oil that is to be added to the milk and lime, and dissolved by a gentle heat. In cold weather, the milk and lime must be warmed, to prevent the pitch from cooling too suddenly, and to enable it to unite more readily with the milk and lime.

Time only can prove how far this mode of painting is to be compared, for durability, with that in oil; for the shrinking to which coatings of paint are subject depends, in great measure, upon the nature and seasoning of the wood.

The milk paint used for in-door work dries in about an hour; and the oil which is employed in preparing it entirely loses its smell in the soapy state to which it is reduced by its union with the lime. One coating will be sufficient for places that are already covered with any colour, unless the latter penetrate through it and produce spots. One coat will likewise suffice, in general, for ceilings and staircases; two will be necessary for new wood.

Milk-painting may be coloured, like every other in distemper, by means of the different colouring substances employed in common painting. The quantity I have given in the receipt will be sufficient for one coat to a surface of about twenty-five square yards.

PRACTICE OF VARNISHING AND POLISHING.

Before beginning to varnish, you must fill up any knots or blemishes with cement of the same colour as the ground. Have your varnish in a pan, such as I have before described, with a piece of wire running diametrically across the top, and slackened downwards, to stroke your brush against. Be careful that the brush be clean and free from loose hairs; dip it in the varnish, stroking it across the wire, and give the work a thin regular coat; soon after that another; and so continue; always taking care not to pass the brush twice over the same place in any one coat, as that would render it unequal.

The greatest difficulty of the operation consists in preventing the different strokes of the brush from being visible. To avoid this, let the brush be perfectly flat and as large as the nature of the work will permit. Draw it gently over the surface in taking your strokes, and be careful not to load the brush with too much varnish at once.

Turned articles are always best varnished while in the lathe by means of heat; because the extension of the varnish is then more uniform and the operation facilitates the polishing afterwards.

When varnish is applied to painting in distemper, it is necessary to allow sufficient time to elapse between the application of the distemper and that of the varnish to let the wood become perfectly dry; if this be not done the varnish will penetrate into the size, and at last bring off the coat of colouring beneath along with it, in thin pieces.

For ordinary purposes, shell-lac varnish does not require to be rubbed down and polished; but when it is wished to produce a very even surface, these processes are necessary: for rubbing down, pumice-stone in fine powder is used. A piece of woollen rag is made wet, and a portion of the powder put upon it; this is rubbed carefully and equally over every part of the varnished surface until it appear perfectly even. Great care is requisite to avoid rubbing through at some parts before others are rendered smooth, particularly if there are sharp edges or projecting mouldings. When this takes place, the whole process of varnishing must be repeated. A little practice will, however, enable any one to avoid this, provided the article varnished have an even surface and the number of coats have been sufficient to give the requisite thickness of resin. When the surface to be polished is flat, the cloth may, when used, be wrapped round a piece of cork or wood; and the same method may be adopted in rubbing down mouldings.

When a surface is well prepared by the pumice-stone, it is very easily polished. This is effected by fine rotten-stone, used exactly in the same way as the pumice-stone, excepting that sweet oil is used instead of water. The oil may be removed from the surface by a fine rag and some dry rotten-stone; and if a little be then rubbed on by the palm of the hand, this will give a high polish to the surface.

The gloss upon the shell-lac which has been polished is less brilliant than that of the unpolished varnish, but this gloss may be given by using a coat of seed-lac varnish, which will abstract but little from the perfect surface given by polishing.

In some cases, hard bodies may be allowably employed in polishing varnishes, but only when these varnishes are themselves hard, such as those resulting from the solution of amber and copal in drying oil, or even in oil of turpentine.

When it is required to clean and polish old furniture, first wash it thoroughly with hot *soft* water to get the dirt off; then take a quart of stale beer or vinegar, put in a handful of common salt and a tablespoonful of spirits of salt, and boil it for a quarter of an hour; keep it in a bottle, and warm it when wanted for use. This mixture should be applied as long as necessary after the furniture has been washed with the hot water.

French Polish.

There is a mode of using shell-lac varnish which is sometimes denominated the German, but more commonly the French mode. It merits to be generally known, as the process is easy and economical, and the effect beautiful. It has been much employed by cabinet and musical instrument makers, but is not yet so extensively practiced as it merits to be.

The varnish is applied by means of what is called a rubber, made by rolling up a piece of thick woollen cloth, which has been *torn* off so as to have a soft, elastic edge. The varnish, put into a narrow-mouthed bottle, is applied to the middle of the flat face of the rubber by laying the rubber on the mouth of the bottle and quickly shaking the varnish at once, as the rubber will thus imbibe a sufficient quantity to varnish a considerable extent of surface. The rubber is then enclosed in a soft linen cloth doubled, the remainder of the cloth being gathered together at the back of the rubber to form a handle to hold it by; and the face of the linen cloth must be moistened with a little raw linseed-oil, which may either be coloured with alkanet root or not, applied with the finger to the middle of it.

The work to be varnished should be placed opposite to the light in order that the effect of the polishing may be better seen, and a surface of from ten to eight feet square may be varnished at once.

The rubber must be quickly and lightly rubbed upon the surface of the article to be varnished, and the rubbing continued until the varnish becomes nearly dry. The coil of woollen cloth must then be again wetted with the varnish (no more oil need be applied to the surface of the linen cloth), and the rubbing renewed till the varnish becomes nearly dry as before; a third coat must be applied in the same manner, then a fourth with a little oil, which must be followed by two others without oil as before. You proceed thus until the varnish has acquired some thickness, which will be after a few repetitions of the series. Apply then a little alcohol to the inside of the linen cloth, and wet the coil with the varnish; after which, rub very quickly, lightly, and uniformly, over every part of the varnished surface, which will tend to make it even, and very much conduce to its polish. The linen cloth must now be wetted with a little alcohol and oil, without varnish. And the varnished surface being rubbed over, with the precautions last mentioned, until it is nearly dry, the effect of the operation will be seen. If it be found not complete, the process must be continued, with the introduction of alcohol in its turn as directed before, until the surface becomes smooth and of a beautiful lustre.

The preceding process is that in general use, but Dr. Jones recommends, in the *Franklin Journal*, a rubber of a different sort, as well as a simpler mode of employing it. He takes a piece of thick woollen cloth six or eight inches in diameter, and upon one side of this pours a teaspoonful of the varnish; he then collects the edges together, so as to enclose the varnish in the cloth and form a handle by which to hold it; this is finally covered with a piece of oiled linen cloth, and the rubber is ready for use. More varnish is added as often as it is required; and when it becomes occasionally too thick to ooze through, a little alcohol is poured into the cloth.

Some difficulties may be at first experienced in performing this process, but Dr. Jones states that a very little practice will enable any handy person to surmount them. The peculiar advantage said to attend it is, that a beautiful polish may be at once obtained by a continued application of the rubber in this way; while, according to the method previously described, successive coats of varnish which require considerable time to dry must be used, and a great deal of additional trouble incurred.

In varnishing recesses or carved work, where parts of the surface are difficult to reach with the rubber, a spirit varnish made with or without lac of the usual gum resins, and considerably thicker than that used for the rest of the work, may be applied to those parts with a brush or hair pencil.

Waxing.

In some instances, the application of wax merely is preferred to any varnish; particularly in the case of chairs, tables, &c., of walnut-tree wood, in daily use.

Waxing resists percussion and friction, but it does not possess, in the same degree as varnish, the property of giving lustre to the bodies to which it is applied, and of heightening their tints. The lustre created by wax is but dull, but this inconvenience is balanced by the ease with which any accidents that may have affected its polish can be replaced by rubbing it with a piece of fine cork.

In waxing, it is of great importance to make the coating as thin as possible, in order that the veins of the wood may be more distinctly seen. I consider the following preparation the best for performing this operation :—

Put two ounces of white and yellow wax over a moderate fire, in a very clean vessel, and, when it is quite melted, add four ounces of the best spirits of turpentine. Stir the whole until it is entirely cool, and you will have a pomade fit for waxing furniture, which must be rubbed over it according to the usual method. The oil soon penetrates the pores of the wood, brings out the colour of it, causes the wax to adhere better, and produce a lustre equal to that of varnish, without being subject to any of its inconveniences.

PRACTICE OF GILDING.

Gilding Carved Wood with Water-Size.

Mix with your preparatory size a sufficient portion of good glue, boiling hot, and lay it upon the wood with a brush, the bristles of which are short. Then apply six, eight, or ten coats, equal in quantity, of the white coating, and be particularly careful that the projecting parts are well covered, as the beauty of the burnish on the gold depends much on this. The first coat should be laid on quite hot, dabbing it with the brush in such a way that it may not be thicker in one place than another. The lower parts of the carving must be covered by dabbing it with a smaller brush. After putting on one coat of white and before following it with a second, the work should be examined, any lumps in it reduced, and small hollows filled up by a cement consisting of whiting and glue kneaded together. Let the whole be now rubbed with fish-skin, which will remove every sort of roughness. The second, third, and remaining coats of white should have the size stronger than in the first coat, yet all of the same strength, otherwise a strong superior coat will cause a weaker one under it to scale off: the operation of dabbing with the brush must be repeated in every successive coat, in order to unite the whole, so that they may form a single compact body.

Each coat must also be perfectly dry before a new one is laid on. The whitened surface is now to be wetted with the brush which has been used for putting on the whiting, dipped in fresh cool water. Only a small portion should be wetted at once, which should then be rubbed down with pumice-stone, made flat for the parts which require to be of that form, and round or hollow, as may be necessary, for the mouldings. Little sticks are used for clearing out those members of the mouldings which may have been filled up by the whiting. The whitened parts are to be rubbed lightly, so as to render the surface smooth and even to the touch. At the same time, a brush which has become soft by using it with the whiting is employed to clear out all the dirt which has been found in the rubbing. The moisture is now to be dried up with a sponge, and any small grains which may remain removed by the finger—a delicate and very important operation. The whole work is finally to be wiped with a piece of clean linen.

The work should now be returned to the carver, to have the fine and delicate cutting of the sculptured parts restored. If the workman be skilful, he will be able to re-produce on the whiting every characteristic trait which may happen to have been obliterated. Where bas-reliefs cast from moulds are laid on a flat or carved surface, instead of the wood itself being carved, as is now very commonly the case, this repairing process is unnecessary.

A moistened cloth is now to be passed over the parts which are to be matted or burnished, and a soft moistened brush over those which have been repaired. The whole is then to be washed with a soft sponge, and every speck and hair carefully removed. All the even parts should next be smoothed with rushes, taking care not to rub off the whiting. The colouring yellow is now to be applied very hot, with a soft clean brush, so as to cover the whole work. This application must be lightly made, so as not to disturb the whiting. The yellow tint serves to cover those deep recesses into which the gold cannot be made to enter: it serves also as a mordant for the gold-size. When this yellow covering becomes dry, the whole surface is to be again gently rubbed with rushes, to remove all specks or hairs which may be found on it, and to give a uniform surface without the slightest inequality.

The gold-size, which is the next thing to apply, you must temper by mixing it with some parchment-size that has been passed through a fine sieve. It is to be laid on warm, with a small brush, the bristles of which are fine, long, and soft: there are brushes made for the express purpose. Three coats of the size will be sufficient. It is to be applied generally to the work, but you need not force it into the deeper parts. When the three coats of size are quite dry, the larger and smoother parts, which are intended to appear matted, are to be rubbed with a piece of new dry linen: this will cause the gold to extend itself evenly, and the water to flow over the sized surface without forming spots. To those parts which are not thus rubbed, but which are intended to be burnished, you must apply two additional coats of the same tempered gold-size, to which a little water has been added to render it thinner.

The work is now ready for Gilding.—Take a book of leaf gold, place the leaves upon a cushion, cut them to the required size, and lay them on the work by means of hair pencils of different sizes; first wetting the part (but that only) on which the gold is to be applied with fresh and cool water. The deep recesses should be gilt before the more prominent parts. When the leaf is deposited in its place, water is applied, to make it spread easily, by means of a pencil behind it, but so as it may not flow, as this would occasion spots; it should also be breathed on gently, and any waste water removed with the point of a pencil.

Those parts of the gilding which it is wished to preserve of a matted appearance should have a slight coat of parchment-size, which will prevent the gold from rubbing off. The size should be warm, but not hot, and its strength half as great as that used with the colouring yellow.

The parts to which it is desired to give a more brilliant appearance are burnished with a burnisher made of wolves' or dogs' teeth, or agate, mounted in iron or wooden handles, which must be kept, throughout the process, perfectly dry. The operation of burnishing is very simple. Take hold of the tool near to the tooth or stone, and lean very hard with it on those parts which are to be burnished, causing it to glide by a backward and forward movement, without once taking it off the piece. When it is requisite that the hand should pass over a large surface at once, without losing its point of support on the work-bench, the workman, on taking hold of the burnisher, should place it just underneath his little finger; by this means, the work is done quicker, and the tool is more solidly fixed in the hand.

It will sometimes happen in gilding that small spots on the deeper parts are overlooked, or that the gold is removed in some parts in applying the matting-size. When this is the case, small pieces of leaf gold are to be put on by means of a pencil, after moistening the deficient places with a small brush; when dry, each of these spots should be covered with a little size.

When it is desired to give the work the appearance of *or moulu*, dip a small fine pencil into the vermilioning composition, and apply it delicately into the indentations and such other parts, where it will, by being reflected, give a good effect to the gold.

To bind and finish the work well, a second coat of the matting size should be passed over the matted parts, and hotter than the first.

Gilding Plaster or Marble with Water-Size.

The chief difference to be observed when plaster or marble has to be gilt instead of wood, is to exclude the salt from the composition of the preparatory size, as in damp situations this would produce a white efflorescence upon the surface of the gold. Two coats of this size should be laid on; the first weak, that it may sink into the plaster or marble and moisten it perfectly; the second, strong.

Gilding Wood in Oil.

The wood must first be covered, or primed, with two or three coatings of boiled linseed oil and carbonate of lead; and when dry, a thin coating of gold oil-size laid upon it. In about twelve hours this sizing, if good, will be dry; when you may begin to apply the gold-leaf, dividing it, and laying it on in the same manner as in the case of the water-gilding, with this difference, that it is to be gently pressed down with a ball of soft cotton; when it will instantly adhere so firmly to the size, that, after a few minutes, the gentle application of a large camel's-hair brush will sweep away all the loose particles of the leaf without disturbing the rest.

The advantages of this oil-gilding are, that it is easily and quickly done, is very durable, is not readily injured by changes of weather, even when exposed to the open air; and when soiled, may be cleaned by a little warm water and a soft brush. It cannot, however, be burnished, and is, therefore, deficient in lustre.

To gild Steel.

Pour some of the ethereal solution of gold into a wine-glass, and dip into it the blade of a new penknife, lancet, or razor; withdraw the instrument, and allow the ether to evaporate: the blade will then be found covered with a beautiful coat of gold. The blade may be moistened with a clean rag, or a small piece of very dry sponge dipped into the ether, and the same effect will be produced.

To gild Copper, Brass, &c.

The gilding of these inferior metals and alloys of them is effected by the assistance of mercury, with which the gold is amalgamated. The mercury is evaporated, while the gold is fixed, by the application of heat; the whole is then burnished, or left mat, in whole or in part, according as required.

In the large way of gilding, the furnaces are so contrived that the volatilized mercury is again condensed, and preserved for further use, so that there is no loss in the operation. There is also a contrivance by which the volatile particles of mercury are prevented from injuring the gilders.

Gilding Glass and Porcelain.

Dissolve in boiled linseed oil an equal weight either of copal or amber, and add as much oil of turpentine as will enable you to apply the compound or size thus formed, as thin as possible, to the parts of the glass intended to be gilt. The glass is to be placed in a stove till it is so warm as almost to burn the fingers when handled. At this temperature the size becomes adhesive, and a piece of leaf gold, applied in the usual way, will immediately stick. Sweep off the superfluous portions of the leaf; and when quite cold it may be burnished, taking care to interpose a piece of India paper between the gold and the burnisher.

It sometimes happens, when the varnish is not very good, that by repeated washing the gold wears off; on this account the practice of burning it in is sometimes had recourse to. For this purpose, some gold-powder is ground with borax, and in this state applied to the clean surface of the glass by a camel's-hair pencil; when quite dry, the glass is put into a stove, heated to about the temperature of an annealing oven; the gum burns off, and the borax, by vitrifying, cements the gold with great firmness to the glass; after which it may be burnished.

The gilding upon porcelain is in like manner fixed by heat and the use of borax; and this kind of ware being neither transparent nor liable to soften, and thus to be injured in its form in a low red heat, is free from the risk and injury which the finer and more fusible kinds of glass are apt to sustain from such treatment. Porcelain and other wares may be platinized, silvered, tinned, or bronzed, in a similar manner.

Gilding Leather.

In order to impress gilt figures, letters, and other marks upon leather, as on the covers of books, edgings for doors, &c., the leather must first be dusted over with very finely-powdered yellow resin, or mastick gum. The iron tools, or stamps, are then arranged on a rack before a clear fire, so as to be well heated, without becoming red hot. If the tools are *letters,* they have an alphabetical arrangement on the rack. Each letter or stamp must be tried as to its heat, by imprinting its mark on the raw side of a piece of waste leather. A little practice will enable the workman to judge of the heat. The tool is now to be pressed downwards on the gold-leaf, which will of course be indented and show the figure imprinted on it. The next letter or stamp is now to be taken and stamped in like manner, and so on with the others; taking care to keep the letters in an even line with each other, like those in a book. By this operation the resin is melted; consequently the gold adheres to the leather. The superfluous gold may then be rubbed off by a cloth, the gilded impressions remaining on the leather. In this as in every other operation, adroitness is acquired by practice.

The cloth alluded to should be slightly greasy to retain the gold wiped off (otherwise there will be a great waste in a few months); the cloth will thus be soon completely saturated or loaded with the gold. When this is the case, these clothes are generally sold to the refiners, who burn them and recover the gold. Some of these afford so much gold by burning as to be worth from a guinea to a guinea and a half.

Gilding Writings, Drawings, &c., on Paper or Parchment.

Letters written on vellum or paper are gilded in three ways. In the first, a little size is mixed with the ink, and the letters are written as usual; when they are dry, a slight degree of stickiness is produced by breathing on them, upon which the gold-leaf is immediately applied, and by a little pressure may be made to adhere with sufficient firmness. In the second method, some white lead or chalk is ground up with strong size, and the letters are made with this by means of a brush. When the mixture is almost dry, the gold-leaf may be laid on, and afterwards burnished. The third method is to mix up some gold-powder with size, and to form the letters of this by means of a brush.

Gilding the Edges of Paper.

The edges of the leaves of books and letter paper are gilded whilst in a horizontal position in the bookbinder's press, by first applying a composition formed of four parts of Armenian bole and one of candied sugar, ground together with water to a proper consistence and laid on by a brush with the white of an egg. This coating, when nearly dry, is smoothed by the burnisher. It is then slightly moistened by a sponge dipped in clean water, and squeezed in the hand. The gold-leaf is now taken up on a piece of cotton, from the leathern cushion, and applied on the moistened surface. When dry, it is to be burnished by rubbing the burnisher over it repeatedly from end to end, taking care not to wound the surface by the point.

ON LACQUERING.

The general nature of the compositions employed for lacquering has already been explained under the head of Changing Varnishes. I shall in this place give some particular receipts for preparing the lacquers in most general use.

Lacquer for Brass.

Seed-lac, six ounces; amber or copal, ground on porphyry or very clean marble, two ounces; dragon's blood, forty grains; extract of red sandal-wood, thirty-grains; oriental saffron, thirty-six grains; pounded glass, four ounces; very pure alcohol, forty ounces.

Articles, or ornaments of brass, to which this varnish is to be applied, should be exposed to a gentle heat and then dipped into the varnish. Two or three coatings may be thus applied, if necessary.

Articles varnished in this manner may be cleaned with water and a bit of dry rag.

Lacquer for Philosophical Instruments.

Gamboge, an ounce and a half; gum sandrac, four ounces; gum elemi, four ounces; best dragon's blood, two ounces; terra merita,* an ounce and a half; oriental saffron, four grains; seed-lac, two ounces; pounded glass, six ounces; pure alcohol, forty ounces.

The dragon's blood, gum elemi, seed-lac, and gamboge are all pounded and mixed with the glass. Over them is poured the tincture obtained by infusing the saffron and terra merita in the alcohol for twenty-four hours. This tincture, before being poured over the dragon's blood, &c., should be strained through a piece of clean linen cloth, and strongly squeezed.

If the dragon's blood gives too high a colour, the quantity may be lessened according to circumstances. The same is the case with the other colouring matters.

This lacquer has a very good effect when applied to many cast or moulded articles used in ornamenting furniture.

Gold-coloured Lacquer for Brass Watch-cases, Watch-keys, &c.

Seed-lac, six ounces; amber, two ounces; gamboge, two ounces; extract of red sandal-wood in water, twenty-four grains; dragon's blood, sixty grains; oriental

---

* Terra merita is the root of an Indian plant; it is of a red colour, and much used in dyeing. In varnishing, it is only employed in the form of a tincture, and is particularly well adapted for the mixture of those colouring parts which contribute the most towards giving metals the colour of gold. In choosing it, be careful to observe that it is sound and compact.

saffron, thirty-six grains; pounded glass, four ounces; pure alcohol, thirty-six ounces.

The seed-lac, amber, gamboge, and dragon's blood must be pounded very fine on porphyry or clean marble, and mixed with the pounded glass. Over this mixture is poured the tincture formed by infusing the saffron and the extract of sandal-wood into the alcohol, in the manner directed in the last receipt. The varnishing is completed as before.

Metal articles that are to be covered with this varnish are heated, and, if they are of a kind to admit of it, are immersed in packets. The tint of the varnish may be varied in any degree required, by altering the proportions of the colouring quantities according to circumstances.

To make Lacquer of various Tints.

For this purpose, make use of the receipt given under the head of Changing Varnishes.

To clean old Brass Work for Lacquering.

First boil a strong lye of wood-ashes, which you may strengthen with soap-lees; put in your brass work, and the lacquer will immediately come off; then have ready a pickle of aqua-fortis and water, strong enough to take off the dirt; wash it immediately in clean water, dry it well, and lacquer it.

BRONZING.

This art is nothing but a species of painting; but far from being of the most delicate kind. The principal ingredients made use of in it are the true gold-powder, the German gold, the aurum mosaicum, (all before described), and copper-powder. This last may be procured by dissolving filings or slips of copper with nitrous acid in a receiver. When the acid is saturated, the slips are to be removed; or if filings be employed, the solution is to be poured off from what remains undissolved. Small bars are then put in, which will precipitate the copper from the saturated acid, in a powder of the peculiar appearance and colour of copper; and the liquid being poured from the powder, this is to be washed clean off the crystals by repeated levigations.

The choice of these powders is, of course, to be determined by the degree of brilliancy you wish to obtain. The powder is mixed with strong gum-water or isinglass, and laid on with a brush or pencil: or, a coating of gold-size, prepared with a due proportion of turpentine, is first applied; and when not so dry as to have still a certain clamminess, a piece of soft leather, wrapped round the finger, is dipped in the powder and rubbed over the work. When the work has, in either of these ways, been all covered with the bronze, it must be left to dry, and any loose powder then cleared away by a hair pencil.

Bronzing in wood may be effected by a process somewhat differing from the above. Prussian blue, patent yellow, raw umber, lamp-black, and pipe-clay, are ground separately with water on a stone, and as much of them as will make a good colour put into a small vessel, three-fourths full of size, not quite so strong as what is called clean size. This mixture is found to succeed best on using about half as much more pipe-clay as of any of the other ingredients. The wood being previously cleaned and smoothed, and coated with a mixture of clean size and lamp-black, receives a new coating with the above compound twice successively, having allowed the first to dry. Afterwards the bronze-powder is to be laid on with a pencil, and the whole burnished or cleaned anew, observing to repair the parts which may be injured by this operation. Next, the work must be coated over with a thin lather of Castile soap, which will take off the glare of the burnishing; and afterwards be carefully rubbed with a woollen cloth. The superfluous powder may be rubbed off when dry.

In *bronzing iron*, the subject should be heated to a greater degree than the hand can bear; and German gold, mixed with a small quantity of spirit-of-wine varnish, spread over it with a pencil. Should the iron be already polished, you must heat it well and moisten it with a linen rag dipped in vinegar.

There is a method of bronzing casts of plaster of Paris analogous to that which we have above given for bronzing wood; but it is not in much repute. Such figures may be beautifully varnished by means of the following composition, recommended by Dr. Johns, of Manchester, England, in the *Mechanics' Magazine*, vol. iv. pp. 303, 352. Of white soap and white wax, take each half an ounce; of water, two pints; boil them together for a short time in a clean vessel. This varnish is to be applied when cold, by means of a soft brush. It does not sink in; it readily dries; and its effect may be heightened by lightly using a silk pocket handkerchief.

JAPANNING.

All wood work intended to be japanned must be prepared with size, and some coarse material mixed with it to fill up and harden the grain of the wood (such as may best suit the colour intended to be laid on), which must be rubbed smooth with glass paper when dry. In cases of accident, it is seldom necessary to re-size the damaged places, unless they are considerable.

Be very careful, in japanning, to grind your colours smooth in spirit of turpentine; then add a small quantity of turpentine and spirit varnish; lay it carefully on with a camel-hair brush, and varnish it with brown or white spirit varnish, according to the colour.

Colours required in Japanning.

Flake white, red lead, vermilion, lake, Prussian blue, patent yellow, orpiment, ochres, verditers, Vandyke brown, umber, lamp-black, and siennas raw and burnt. With these you may match almost any colours in general use in japanning. For a black japan, it will be found sufficient to mix a little gold-size with lamp-black; this will bear a good gloss, without requiring to be varnished afterwards.

To prepare a fine Tortoise-shell Japan ground by means of Heat.

Take one gallon of good linseed oil, and half a pound of umber; boil them together till the oil becomes very brown and thick: then strain it through a coarse cloth, and set it again to boil; in which state it must be continued till it acquire a consistence resembling that of pitch; it will then be fit for use.

Having thus prepared the varnish, clean well the substance which is to be japanned. Then lay vermilion tempered with shell-lac varnish or with drying oil very thinly diluted with oil of turpentine, on the places intended to imitate the more transparent parts of the tortoise-shell. When the vermilion is dry, brush the whole over with black varnish, tempered to a due consistence with the oil of turpentine. When set and firm, put the work into a stove, where it may undergo a very strong heat, which must be continued a considerable time; if even three weeks or a month, it will be the better.

This tortoise-shell ground is not less valuable for its great hardness, and enduring to be made hotter than boiling water without damage, than for the superior beauty and brilliancy of its appearance.

FOILS.

Foils are thin plates or leaves of metal that are put under stones, or compositions in imitation of stones, when they are set, either to increase the lustre and play of the stones, or more generally to improve the colour, by giving an additional force to the tinge, whether it be natural or artificial, by a ground of the same hue.

There are two kinds of foils. One is colourless, where the effect of giving lustre to the stone is produced by the polish of the surface, making it act as a mirror, and, by reflecting the light, preventing the deadness which attends a duller ground under the stone, and bringing it nearer to the effect of the diamond. The other is coloured with some pigment or stain, either of the same hue as the stone, or of some other, which is intended to change the hue of the stone in some degree; thus, a yellow foil may be put under green which is too much inclined to blue, or under crimson, where it is desired to have the appearance of orange or scarlet.

Foils may be made of copper or tin. Silver has been sometimes used, and even gold mixed with it; but the expense of either is needless, as copper may be made to answer the same end.

Copper intended for foils is prepared by taking copper plates beaten to a proper thickness, passing them betwixt a pair of fine steel rollers very closely set, and drawing them as thin as possible. They are polished with very fine whiting, or rotten-stone, till they shine, and have as much brightness as can be given them, and they will then be fit to receive the colour. If they are intended for a purple or crimson colour, the foils should first be whitened in the following manner: Take a small quantity of silver, and dissolve it in *aqua-fortis;* then put bits of copper into the solution, and precipitate the silver; which being done, the fluid must be poured off, and fresh water added to it to wash away all the remainder of the first fluid; after which the silver must be dried, and an equal weight of cream of tartar and common salt ground with it, till the whole is reduced to a very fine powder. With this mixture, the foils, slightly moistened, must be rubbed by the finger, or a bit of linen rag, till they are of the degree of whiteness desired.

The manner of preparing foils, so as to give colourless stones the greatest degree of play and lustre, by raising so high a polish or smoothness on the surface as in many instances to nearly resemble the effect of diamonds, I shall not here detail, as it is not one in which the general occupations of the Painter, Varnisher, or Gilder, would be of assistance. The method of colouring these substances I shall here describe.

To colour Foils.

Two methods have been invented for colouring foils; the one by tinging the surface of the copper with the colour required by means of smoke, the other by staining or painting it with some colouring substance.

The colours used for painting foils may be mixed with either oil, water rendered glutinous by gum-arabic, size, or varnish. Where deep colours are wanted, oil is most proper, because some pigments become wholly transparent in it, as lake or Prussian blue: the yellow and green may be better laid on in varnish, as these colours may be had in perfection from a tinge wholly dissolved in spirit of wine, in the same manner as in the case of lacquers; and the most beautiful green is to be produced by distilled verdigris, which is apt to lose its colour and turn black with oil. In common cases, however, any of the colours may be, with the least trouble, laid on with isinglass-size, in the same manner as the glazing colours used in miniature painting.

Where the *ruby* is to be imitated, a little lake used in isinglass size, carmine, or shell-lac varnish, is to be employed, if the glass or paste be of a full crimson, verging towards the purple; but if the glass incline to the scarlet, or orange, very bright lake, not purple, may be used alone in oil.

For *garnet red*, dragon's blood dissolved in seed-lac varnish may be used; and for the *vinegar garnet*, the orange lake, tempered with shell-lac varnish, will be found excellent.

For the *amethyst*, lake, with a little Prussian blue, used with oil, and very thinly spread on the foil, will answer.

For *blue*, where a deep colour or sapphire is wanted,

Prussian blue, not too deep, should be used in oil, and be spread more or less thinly on the foil, according to the lightness or deepness of the colour required.

For *eagle marine*, common verdigris, with a little Prussian blue, tempered in shell-lac varnish.

Where a *full yellow* is desired, the foil may be coloured with a yellow lacquer, laid on as for other purposes. For *light yellows*, the copper ground of the foil itself, properly burnished, will be sufficient.

For *green*, where a deep hue is required, the crystals of verdigris, tempered in shell-lac varnish, should be used; but where the *emerald* is to be imitated, a little yellow lacquer should be added, to bring the colour to a truer green, and less verging to the blue.

The stones of more diluted colour, such as the *amethyst, topaz, vinegar-garnet*, and *eagle marine*, may be very cheaply imitated by transparent white glass or paste, even without foils. This is to be done by tempering the colours above mentioned with turpentine and mastic, and painting the socket in which the counterfeit stone is to be set with the mixture, the socket and stone itself being previously heated. In this case, however, the stone should be immediately set, and the socket closed upon it before the mixture cools and grows hard. The orange lake, mentioned under the head of garnet red, was invented for this purpose, in which it has a beautiful effect, and has been used with great success. The colour it produces is that of the vinegar-garnet, which it affords with great brightness.

The colours before directed to be used in oil should

be extremely well ground in oil of turpentine, and tempered with oil—nut or poppy oil; or, if time can be given for their drying, with strong fat oil, diluted with spirits of turpentine, which will gain a fine polish of itself. The colours used in varnish should be likewise thoroughly well ground and mixed; and in the case of dragon's blood in the seed-lac varnish and the lacquer, the foils should be warmed before they are laid out. All the mixtures should be laid on the foils with a broad soft brush, which must be passed from one end to the other, and no part should be crossed or twice gone over —or at least not till the first coat be dry; when, if the colour does not lie enough, a second coat may be given.

FISH OIL COLOURS.

Various coarse paints, applicable to out-door work, and of great cheapness and durability, may be made with fish oil, according to the following processes:—

To prepare the Oil.

Into a cask which will contain about forty gallons, put thirty-two gallons of good common vinegar; add to this twelve pounds of litharge, and twelve pounds of white copperas in powder: bung up the vessel, and shake and roll it well twice a-day for a week, when it will be fit to put into a ton of whale, cod, or seal oil (but the Southern whale oil is to be preferred, on account of its good colour and little or no smell): shake and mix all together, when it may settle until the next day; then pour off the clear, which will be about seven-eighths of the whole. To clear this part, add twelve gallons of linseed oil, and two gallons of spirit of turpentine; shake them well together, and, after the whole has settled two or three days, it will be fit to grind white lead and all fine colours in; and, when ground, cannot be distinguished from those ground in linseed oil, unless by the superiority of colour.

If the oil be wanted only for coarse purposes, the linseed oil and oil of turpentine may be added at the same time that the prepared vinegar is put in; and, after being well shaken up, is fit for immediate use, without being suffered to settle.

The residue or bottom, when settled by the addition of half its quantity of fresh lime-water, forms an excellent oil for mixing with all the coarse paints for preserving outside work.

All colours ground in the above oil, and used for inside work, must be thinned with linseed oil and oil of turpentine.

Gain by the above process.

One ton of fish oil, or 252 gallons	$151 20
32 gallons of vinegar, at 12½ cents per gallon	4 00
12 lbs. litharge, at 7 cts. per lb.	84
12 lbs. white copperas, at 8 cts. ditto	96
12 gallons of linseed oil, at 90 cts. per gallon	10 80
2 gallons of spirit of turpentine, at 40 cts.	80
	$168 60

252 gallons of fish oil
 12 ditto linseed oil
  2 ditto spirit of turpentine
 32 ditto vinegar

298 gallons, at 90 cts. per gallon $268 20

Deduct the expense . . 168 60

$99 60

Preparations and Cost of particular Colours.

I.—*Subdued Green.*

Fresh lime-water, 6 gallons	$ 06
Road dirt finely sifted, 112 pounds	10
Whiting, 112 ditto	1 12
Blue-black, 30 ditto	1 50
Wet blue, 20 ditto	4 00
Residue of the oil, 3 gallons	1 50
Yellow ochre in powder, 24 pounds	1 20
	$9 48

This composition will weigh three hundred and sixty-eight pounds, which is little more than two and a half cents per pound. To render the above paint fit for use, to every eight pounds add one quart of the incorporated oil, and one quart of linseed oil, and it will be found a paint with every requisite quality, as well of beauty as of durability, and cheapness, and in this state of preparation does not cost five cents per pound.

The following is the mode of mixing the ingredients:—

First pour six gallons of lime-water into a large tub, then throw in one hundred and twelve pounds of whiting; stir it round well with a stirrer, let it settle for about an hour, and stir it again. The painter may then put in the one hundred and twelve pounds of road dirt, mix it well, and add the blue-black, after which the yellow ochre; and when all is tolerably blended, take it out of the tub, and put it on a large board or platform, and with a labourer's shovel mix and work it about as they do mortar. Now add the wet blue, which must be previously ground in the incorporated oil (as it will not grind or mix with any other oil). When this is added to the mass, you may begin to thin it with the incorporated oil, in the proportion of one quart to every eight pounds, and then the linseed oil in the same proportion, and it is ready to be put into casks for use.

II.—*Lead Colour*.

Whiting, 112 pounds	$1 12
Blue-black, 5 ditto	25
Lead ground in oil, 28 ditto	2 24
Road dirt, 56 ditto	10
Lime-water, 5 gallons	05
Residue of the oil, 2¼ ditto	1 25
Weighs 256 pounds.	$5 01

To the above add two gallons of the incorporated oil, and two gallons of linseed oil to thin it for use, and it will not exceed two cents and a quarter.

The lime-water, whiting, road dirt, and blue-black must be first mixed together; then add the ground lead, first blending it with two gallons and a half of the prepared fish oil; after which, thin the whole with the two gallons of linseed oil and two gallons of incorporated oil, and it will be fit for use. For garden doors, and other work liable to be in constant use, a little spirits of turpentine may be added to the paint whilst laying on, which will have the desired effect.

III.—*Bright Green.*

112 pounds yellow ochre in powder, at 5 cents per pound	$5 60
168 ditto road dust	25
112 ditto wet blue, at 20 cts. per pound	22 40
10 ditto blue-black, at 5 cts. ditto	50
6 gallons of lime-water	06
4 ditto fish oil, prepared	2 40
7½ ditto incorporated oil	4 28
7½ ditto linseed oil, at 90 cts. per gallon	6 75
592 pounds weight	$42 24

It will be seen that the bright green costs but about seven cents per pound, ready to lay on; and the inventor challenges any colourman or painter to produce a green equal to it for five times the price.

After painting, the colour left in the pot may be covered with water to prevent it from skinning, and the brushes, as usual, should be cleaned with the painting-knife, and kept under water.

A brighter green may be formed by omitting the blue-black.

A lighter green may be made by the addition of ten pounds of ground white lead.

A variety of greens may be obtained by varying the proportions of the blue and yellow.

Observe that the wet blue must be ground with the incorporated oil, preparatory to its being mixed with the mass.

IV.—*Stone Colour.*

Lime-water, 4 gallons	$ 04
Whiting, 112 pounds	1 12
White lead, ground, 28 pounds	2 24
Road dust, 56 pounds	10
Prepared fish oil, 2 gallons	1 20
Incorporated oil, 3½ gallons	2 00
Linseed oil, 3½ ditto	3 15
Weighs 293 pounds	$9 85

The above stone colour, fit for use, is not three and a half cents per pound.

V.—*Brown Red.*

Lime-water, 8 gallons	$ 08
Spanish brown, 112 pounds	3 36
Road dust, 224 pounds	40
4 gallons of fish oil	2 40
4 ditto incorporated oil	2 28
4 ditto linseed oil	3 60
Weighs 501 pounds	$12 12

This paint is scarcely two and a half cents per pound. The Spanish brown must be in powder.

VI.—A good *chocolate colour* is made by the addition of blue-black, in powder, or lamp-black, till the colour is to the painter's mind; and a lighter brown may be formed by adding ground white lead. By ground lead is meant white lead ground in oil.

VII.—*Yellow* is prepared with yellow ochre in powder, in the same proportion as Spanish brown.

VIII.—*Black* is also prepared in the same proportion, using lamp-black or blue-black.

GLASS-STAINING.

In the production of pictures on glass, fragments of coloured glass are used, which are cut in pieces of the proper shape, and united by lead. In this way are formed the ground tints, skies, draperies, ornaments, &c. The shades, heads, hands, &c., are then painted in vitrifiable colours, which, after being laid on, are burnt or fired into the glass. The precaution should be observed in joining the pieces of coloured glass, that the lead joints do not interfere with the effect of the picture. That which characterizes painting on glass, and distinguishes it from painting on porcelain, is that the artist makes use of both surfaces of the glass. The surface placed towards the spectator receives all the shades, which are thus rendered more life like and better defined. All the shading colours are likewise placed on this side; all the lights of the picture are thrown on the other side. By this means colours may be used which would be injured by contact with each other, and the superposition of which would produce peculiar tints not desirable.

The pigments used in painting on glass are principally metallic oxides and chlorides, and as in most of these, the colour is not brought out until after the painting is submitted to heat, it is necessary to ascertain beforehand if the colours are properly mixed, by painting on slips of glass, and exposing them to heat in the muffle. The painter is guided by these trial pieces, in laying on his colours. As the effect of a picture on glass is produced by transmitted and not by reflected light, it is necessary that the colours, after being burnt on, should be more or less transparent.

As the coloured glass which forms the ground on which the artist works is manufactured in glass-works, and is an article of commerce, it is necessary to consider here only the colours which are burnt on in the muffle. The temperature at which these are burnt on is never raised above the melting point of silver.

In oil and water-colour paintings, the pigments are rubbed up with oil, solutions of gum, water, &c. In painting on glass, it is necessary to have a proper vehicle for the colours, which will become liquid at a red heat, and which performs the same function as oils, &c., in ordinary painting. This vehicle is called a *flux*. It envelops the colour which is mechanically mixed with it, and glues it, as it were, to the glass. The colour and the flux are often confounded, however, under the name of *vitrifiable colours*, which are mixtures of colour and flux. The vehicle or flux varies with colour, but these variations are very limited, as the colours ought to be capable of mixing with each other. The flux ordinarily employed is a simple silicate of lead, or a mixture of silicate of lead and borax. Experiment has shown that potash and soda cannot be substituted for borax. The following are the proportions of the ingredients of various fluxes :—

No. 1.

Minium or red lead	3 parts.
White sand washed	1 part.

This mixture is melted, by which it is converted into a greenish-yellow glass.

No. 2.—Gray Flux.

Of No. 1	8 parts.
Fused borax in powder	1 part.

This mixture is melted.

No. 3.—Flux for Carmines and Greens.

Fused borax	5 parts.
Calcined flint	3 "
Pure minium	1 part.

This mixture is also melted.

The various colours used in glass-painting are obtained from the following substances:—

The *blue* on glass is produced with cobalt; the *purples, violets,* and *carmines,* with the purple of Cassius; the *reds, browns,* &c., with the peroxide of iron; the *greens* with the silicate of copper, sometimes with the oxide of chromium (in glass-painting, greens of copper are preferred to those of chromium, on account of their greater transparency), often with a mixture of blue and yellow; the *blacks, grays,* &c., with the oxides of manganese, cobalt, and iron; the *yellows* with the oxide of uranium, the chromate of lead, certain combinations of silver, finally the compounds of antimonious acid, and of oxide of lead, or of the subsulphate of iron.

Beautiful yellow tones may be produced on glass by placing on its surface a layer of three parts of pipe-clay, well burnt and pounded, and rubbed up with one part of chloride of silver. The glass is then submitted to heat in a muffle. After cooling, the layer of clay is removed, and the glass is stained yellow. The tint depends on the nature of the glass and the proportion of chloride of silver. Glass containing about eight or ten per cent. of alumina, takes a more beautiful tint than glass containing only two or three per cent.

The following are some of the colours used in the celebrated porcelain manufactory of Sevres, and the proportions in which they are compounded. These colours, though intended for painting on porcelain, are nearly all applicable to painting on glass.

BLUES are obtained with the silicate of cobalt. The oxide of cobalt must be in the state of silicate, in order that the blue colour be developed. The colour once produced, is unalterable at all temperatures.

No. 1.—*Indigo Blue.*

Oxide of cobalt	1 part.
Flux No. 3	2 parts.

No. 2.—*Turquoise Blue.*

Oxide of cobalt	1 part.
Oxide of zinc	3 or 4 parts.
Flux No. 3	6 "

Melt and pour out. If it is not sufficiently green, increase the zinc and flux.

No. 3.—*Azure Blue.*

Oxide of cobalt	1 part.
Oxide of zinc	2 parts.
Flux No. 2	8 "

Melt them together.

No. 4.—*Deep Azure Blue.*

Oxide of cobalt	1 part.
Oxide of zinc	2 parts.
Flux No. 2	5 "

The beauty of this colour depends on the proportion of flux. As little as possible is to be used; it must, however, be brilliant. Sometimes less is used than the proportion indicated.

No. 5.—*Sky Blue, for the Browns.*

Oxide of cobalt	1 part.
Oxide of zinc	2 parts.
Flux No. 2	12 "

Pound up, melt, and pour out.

No. 6.—*Violet Blue, for ground colour.*

Blue No. 5	4 parts.
Violet of gold, No. 31	2 "

More or less of the violet of gold is added. Triturate without melting.

No. 7.—*Lavender Blue, for ground tint.*

Blue No. 5	4 parts.
Violet of gold, No. 31	3 "

Sometimes a little carmine is added. Pulverize without melting.

GREENS are obtained with the oxide of chromium, or with the deutoxide of copper, or with mixtures of oxide of chromium and silicate of cobalt, when bluish tones are wished. When these greens contain the oxide of copper, they require a previous fusion, for it is only in the state of silicate or of salt that this oxide gives a green. The greens of copper disappear entirely at a high heat.

When the colours are required to be transparent, the oxide of copper is used instead of the oxide of chromium.

No. 8.—*Emerald Green.*

Oxide of copper	1 part.
Antimonic acid	10 parts.
Flux No. 1	30 "

Pulverize together, and melt.

No. 9.—*Bluish Green.*

Green oxide of chromium	1 part.
Oxide of cobalt	2 parts.

Triturate, and melt at a high heat. The product is a button slightly melted, from which is removed the portion in contact with the crucible. This button is pounded up, and three parts of flux No. 3, for one of the button, are added to it.

No. 10.—*Grass Green.*

Green oxide of chromium	1 part.
Flux No. 3	3 parts.

Triturate, and melt.

Nos. 10, 11, 12.—*Dragon, Pistache, and Olive Green.*

They are prepared with the oxide of chromium, mixed with flux No. 3, with additions of deep or clear yellow No. 15 or 16, ascertaining the proportions by trial.

YELLOWS are commonly obtained by means of antimonic acid and the oxide of lead (litharge). It is the Naples yellow, or very nearly so. Sometimes stannic acid (peroxide of tin) is added, and oxide of zinc, and often also some subsulphate of the peroxide of iron, prepared by exposing to the air weak solutions of the protosulphate of iron (copperas).

These colours do not change in the muffle, but they disappear almost entirely at a high heat. They are easily altered by smoke, by which the oxide of lead is reduced, which produces a dirty gray.

Yellows are made with the chromate of lead, but their use is too uncertain. In Germany, the oxide of uranium is employed, which gives a beautiful yellow; but in France, it is found to produce no better yellow than those already known.

No. 13.—*Sulphur Yellow.*

Antimonic acid	1 part.
Subsulphate of the peroxide of iron	8 parts.
Oxide of zinc	4 "
Flux No. 1	36 "

Rub up together, and melt; if this colour is too deep, the salt of iron is diminished.

No. 14.—*Fixed Yellow for touches.*

Yellow No. 13	1 part.
White enamel of commerce	2 parts.

Melt, and pour out. If it is not sufficiently fixed, a little sand may be added.

No. 15.—*Yellow for Browns and Greens.*

Antimonic acid	2 parts.
Subsulphate of iron	1 part.
Flux No. 1	9 parts.

This colour is melted, and sometimes a little Naples yellow is added if it is too soft (*i. e.* melts too easily).

No. 16.—*Deep Yellow, to mix with the Chromium Greens.*

Antimonic acid	2 parts.
Subsulphate of iron	1 part.
Flux No. 1	10 parts.

Melt, and pour out. The subsulphate of iron may be increased a little: the proportions of flux vary.

No. 17.—*Jonquille Yellow for flowers.*

Litharge	18 parts.
Sand	6 "
The product of the calcination of equal parts of lead and tin	2 "
Carbonate of soda	1 part.
Antimonic acid	1 "

Rub together or triturate, and melt.

No. 18.—*Wax Yellow.*

Litharge	18 parts.
Sand	4 "
Oxide of antimony	2 "
Sienna earth	2 "

Melt. If it is too deep, the proportion of Sienna earth may be decreased.

No. 19.—*Fixed Wax Yellow.*

No. 18 mixed, without melting, with white enamel or sand in order to harden it. The quantity depends on the greater or less fusibility of the yellow.

No. 20.—*Nankin Yellow for grounds.*

Subsulphate of iron	1 part.
Oxide of zinc	2 parts.
Flux No. 1	10 "

Triturate.

No. 21.—*Deep Nankin Yellow.*

Subsulphate of iron	1 part.
Oxide of zinc	2 parts.
Flux No. 2	8 "

Triturate without melting.

No. 22.—*Pale Yellow Ochre.*

Subsulphate of iron	1 part.
Oxide of zinc	2 parts.
Flux No. 2	6 "

Triturate without melting.

No. 23.—*Deep Yellow Ochre, called Yellow Brown.*

Subsulphate of iron	1 part.
Oxide of zinc	1 "
Flux No. 2	5 parts.

Triturate without melting.

No. 24.—*Brown Yellow Ochre.*

Yellow ochre, No. 23	10 parts.
Sienna earth	1 part.

Mix without melting.

No. 25.—*Isabella Yellow, for grounds.*

Yellow for browns, No. 15	20 parts.
Blood red, No. 28	1 part.

No. 26.—*Orange Yellow, for grounds.*

Chromate of lead	1 part.
Minium	3 parts.

Melt.

No. 27.—*Brick Red.*

Yellow No. 23	12 parts.
Red oxide of iron	1 part.

No. 28.—*Deep Blood Red.*

Subsulphate of iron, calcined in a muffle until it becomes a beautiful capucine red	1 part.
Flux No. 2	3 parts.

Mix without melting.

COLOURS OF GOLD.—These are carmine reds, purples and violets, made by means of the precipitated purple of Cassius. These colours are very delicate, and are the only ones which change their tints in the fire. Unburnt, they are of dirty violet tint, but are changed into a lively and pure tone by a moderate burning. In a stronger fire, these colours become yellowish, and even completely disappear. It is necessary to mix the purple of Cassius with considerable flux, and this mixture must be made while the purple precipitate is still moist. If it was suffered to dry, the colour would be spoiled. With one part of purple of Cassius, six parts of flux are mixed. The purple powder of Cassius gives a purple by itself. Mixed with chloride of silver, which gives to it a yellow, a carmine tone is produced. With a little cobalt blue, it is rendered violet.

No. 29.—*Hard Carmine.*

It is the purple of Cassius mixed with flux No. 3, and chloride of silver, previously melted with ten parts of flux No. 3. The proportions vary. The whole is ground on a glass, the precipitate of gold being still moist.

No. 30.—*Pure Purple.*

The purple powder of Cassius mixed while moist with flux No. 3, and sometimes a little chloride of silver previously melted with flux No. 3. If the purple when prepared does not melt sufficiently easy, some flux may be added when it is dry.

No. 31.—*Deep Violet.*

The purple of Cassius; in place of flux No. 3, flux No. 1 is mixed with it. Sometimes a little of blue No. 6 is added.

COLOURS OF IRON.—Besides the subsulphate of the peroxide, the peroxide itself is employed to produce rose tints, reds, violet tones, and browns. The pure peroxide can produce the first three tones, and it is easily imagined when we know that its shade varies from rose to deep violet, according to the temperature to which it has been submitted. Slightly heated, it is rose or red; at a forge heat, it becomes violet. As to the browns of iron, they require some mixtures. These colours are unalterable in the muffle, but they disappear in great part at a high heat. In the first case the oxide remains free, and in the second it is united with the silica. A too fusible flux or glass produces the same effect.

No. 32.—*Flesh Red.*

The sulphate of iron, put in small crucibles and lightly calcined, produces a suitable red oxide. Those which have the desired tone are selected. All the flesh reds are made in this way, and vary only in the degrees of heat which they receive.

BROWNS may be obtained with various mixtures of peroxide or subsulphate of iron with the oxide of manganese, silicate of cobalt, or silicate of copper. These colours, unalterable in the heat of the muffle, lose their intensity at a high heat.

No. 33.—*Clove Brown.*

The basis of this brown is yellow ochre No. 23, to which is added either the oxide of cobalt *in small quantities*, or umber or sienna earth. Proportions are tried according to the tone required.

No. 34.—*Wood Brown.*

The same process as the clove brown; only without the oxide of cobalt.

No. 35.—*Hair Brown.*

Yellow ochre, No. 23	15 parts.
Oxide of cobalt	1 part.

Well triturated and calcined, in order to give the tone to it.

No. 36.—*Liver Brown.*

Oxide of iron made of a red brown, and mixed with three times its weight of flux No. 2. A tenth of sienna earth is added to it, if it is not sufficiently deep.

No. 37.—*Sepia Brown.*

Deep yellow ochre	15 parts.
Oxide of cobalt	1 part.

A little manganese is added if it is not sufficiently deep. All the ingredients are well mixed, and calcined in order to produce the tone.

No. 38.—*White.*

The white enamel of commerce in cakes.

No. 39.

Another white is prepared by mixing equal parts of fluxes No. 1 and No. 3.

No. 40.— *Yellowish-Gray for Browns and Reds.*

Yellow, No. 15	1 part.
Blue, No. 5	1 "
Oxide of zinc	2 or 3 parts.
Flux No. 2	5 "

Sometimes a little black is added, according to the tone which the mixture produces. The proportions of the blue and yellow vary.

No. 41.— *Bluish-Gray for Mixtures.*

Blue, previously made by melting together three parts of flux No. 1, and one part of the mixture of

Oxide of cobalt	8 parts.
Oxide of zinc	1 part.
Sulphate of iron calcined at a forge heat	1 "
Flux No. 2	3 parts.

Triturate, and add a little manganese in order to render it more gray.

No. 42.— *Grayish-Black for Mixtures.*

Yellow ochre, No. 23	15 parts.
Oxide of cobalt	1 part.

Triturate and calcine in a crucible until it has the desired tone. A little oxide of manganese is added in order to make it blacker, sometimes a little more of oxide of cobalt.

No. 43.—*Deep Black.*

Oxide of cobalt	2 parts.
" " copper	2 "
" " manganese	2 "
Flux No. 1	6 "
Fused borax	½ part.

Melt, and add

Oxide of manganese	1 "
" " copper	2 parts.

Triturate without melting.

The colours thus prepared, after having been rubbed up on a plate of ground glass with the spirits of turpentine, or lavender, thickened in the air, are applied with a hair pencil. Before using them, however, it is necessary to try them on small pieces of glass, and expose them to the fire, to ascertain if the desired tone of colour is produced. The artist must be guided by these proof pieces in using his colours. The proper glass for receiving these colours should be uniform, colourless, and difficult of fusion. For this reason, crown glass made with a little alkali or kelp is preferred.

A design must be drawn upon paper, and placed beneath the plate of glass; though the artist cannot regulate his tints directly by his palette, but by specimens of the colours producible from his palette pigments after they are fired. The upper side of the glass being sponged over with gum-water, affords, when dry, a surface proper for receiving the colours, without the risk of their running irregularly, as they would be apt to do on the slippery glass. The artist first draws on the plate, with a fine pencil, all the traces which mark the great outlines and shades of the figures. This is usually done in black, or at least some strong colour, such as brown, blue, green, or red. In laying on these, the painter is guided by the same principles as the engraver, when he produces the effect of light and shade, by dots, lines, or hatches; and he employs that colour to produce the shades which will harmonize best with the colour which is afterwards to be applied; but for the deeper shades, black is in general used. When this is finished, the whole picture will be represented in lines or hatches similar to an engraving, finished up to the highest effect possible; and afterwards, when it is dry, the vitrifying colours are laid on by means of larger hair pencils; their selection being regulated by the burnt specimen tints. When he finds it necessary to lay two colours adjoining, which are apt to run together in the muffle, he must apply one of them to the back of the glass. The yellow formed with chloride of silver is generally laid on the back of the glass. After colouring, the artist proceeds to bring out the lighter effects by taking off the colour in the proper place, with a goosequill cut like a pen without a slit. By working this upon the glass, he removes the colour from the parts where the lights should be the strongest; such as the hair, eyes, the reflection of bright surfaces and light parts of draperies.

154   THE PAINTER, GILDER,

The blank pen may be employed either to make the lights by lines, or hatches and dots, as is most suitable to the subject.

To fire the paintings, a furnace with a muffle is used. The muffles are made of refractory clay. They have been made of cast iron, but these are no longer employed. Fig. 4 is an elevation and transverse section of the fur-

Fig. 4.

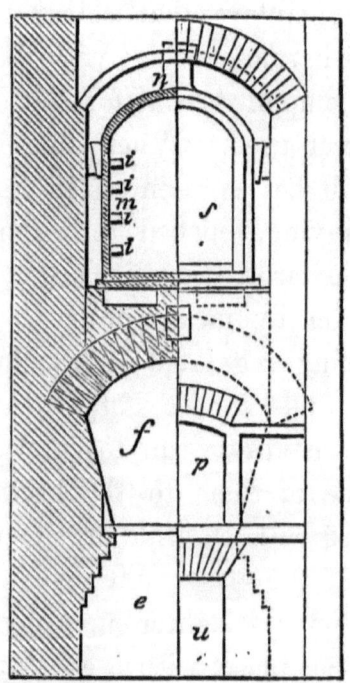

nace, and its muffle in place. Fig. 5 is a longitudinal section. Figs. 6 and 7 views of the muffle; u is the

Fig. 5.

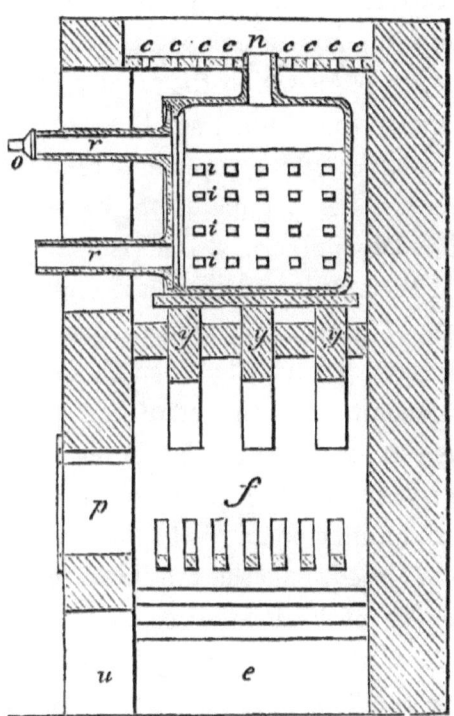

door of the ashpit e, p the door of the furnace f; y, y, are the small arches of the dome of the furnace which

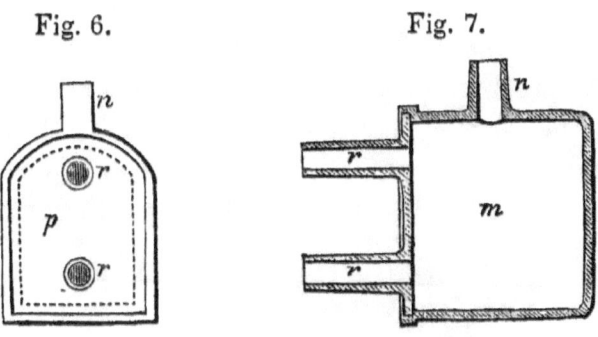

supports the muffle. *c, c* are the flues through which the flame escapes; *n* is a pipe or tube on the top of the muffle to allow vapours to escape; *r, r,* tubes in the door of the muffle, through which the proof pieces are passed. In the interior of the muffle, small brackets or projections *i, i* are placed, which support bars of iron encased in porcelain, on which the plates of glass which are to be burned rest. Dry pulverized lime is sometimes laid on the bottom of the muffle and the glass rested on the lime. Several layers of glass may be placed in the muffle together, with layers of lime between them. This is the better arrangement. As the paintings retain considerable oil, it is necessary, when the muffle is first charged, to heat gently, in order to volatilize or decompose this oil, leaving the muffle open. When the oil is driven off, the muffle is closed, and the fire increased. A greater or less intensity of heat is directed from one part to another of the muffle, by opening or closing the flues *c,* so as to cause the flames to pass over any point desired. The temperature suitable for burning is judged of by placing in the muffle pieces of glass painted with a little carmine. The heat should not be carried beyond the point at which the carmine is well developed. These pieces are fastened to iron wires, by which they may be passed in or out of the muffle through the tubes *r, r.* In this way the progress of the burning may be closely watched. When the carmine is well developed, the fire should be arrested, and the muffle allowed to cool. When the muffle has entirely cooled, the glass is withdrawn. If any parts are defective, they may be re-touched and put in the muffle a second time. Sufficient time should be allowed for the glass to become entirely cool, before withdrawing it.

HARMONY OF COLOURS.

Every one must have observed that certain colours, when brought together, mutually set each other off to advantage, while others have altogether a different effect. This must be carefully attended to by every painter who would study beauty or elegance in the appearance of his work.

Whites will set off well with any colour whatever.

Reds set off best with whites, blacks, or yellows.

Blues with whites or yellows.

Greens with blacks and whites.

Gold sets off well either with blacks or browns.

In lettering or edging with gold, a white ground has a delicate appearance for a time, but it soon becomes dingy. The best grounds for gold are Saxon blue, vermilion, and lake.

MISCELLANEOUS SUBJECTS

AND

USEFUL RECEIPTS.

Though the whole of the following subjects and receipts can not be strictly said to relate to the trades of the Painter, Gilder, or Varnisher, yet most of them are so intimately connected with them, and also so useful to him, that the present Manual could not be considered complete without their being introduced.

To increase the Strength of common Rectified Spirits of Wine, so as to make it equal to that of the best.

Take a pint of the common spirits, and put it into a bottle which it will only fill about three-quarters full. Add to it half an ounce of pearlash or salt of tartar, powdered as much as it can be without occasioning any great loss of its heat. Shake the mixture frequently for about half an hour, before which time a considerable sediment, like phlegm, will be separated from the spirits, and will appear along with the undissolved pearlash or salt at the bottom of the bottle. Then pour the spirit off into another bottle, being careful to bring none of the sediment or salt along with it.* To the quantity just poured off, add half an ounce of pearlash, powdered and heated as before, and repeat the same treatment. Continue to do this as often as you find necessary till you perceive little or no sediment: when this is the case, an ounce of alum, powdered and made hot, but not burned, must be put into the spirits, and suffered to remain some hours, the bottle being frequently shaken during the time; after which the spirit, when poured off, will be found free from all impurities, and equal to the best rectified spirits of wine.

To Silver by Heat.

Dissolve an ounce of pure silver in aqua-fortis, and precipitate it with common salt; to which add, half a pound of sal-ammoniac, sandever, and white vitriol, and a quarter of an ounce of sublimate.

Or dissolve an ounce of pure silver in aqua-fortis, and precipitate it with common salt; and add, after washing, six ounces of common salt, three ounces each of sandever and white vitriol, and a quarter of an ounce of sublimate. These are to be ground into a paste, upon a fine stone, with a muller; the substance to be silvered must be rubbed over with a sufficient quantity of the paste, and

---

* For this purpose, you had better use what is called a *separating funnel*, if you can procure it.

exposed to a proper degree of heat. When the silver runs, it is taken from the fire and dipped into weak spirit of salts to clean it.

To Tin Copper and Brass.

Boil six pounds of cream of tartar, four gallons of water, and eight pounds of grain tin or tin shavings. After the materials have boiled a sufficient time, the substance to be tinned is put therein, and the boiling continued, when the tin is precipitated in its metallic form.

To Tin Iron and Copper Vessels.

Iron which is to be tinned must be previously steeped in acid materials, such as sour whey, distiller's wash, &c.; then scoured and dipped in melted tin, having been first rubbed over with a solution of sal-ammoniac. The surface of the tin is prevented from calcining by covering it with a coat of fat. Copper vessels must be well cleansed; and then a sufficient quantity of tin with sal-ammoniac is put therein, and brought into fusion, and the copper vessel moved about. A little resin is sometimes added. The sal-ammoniac prevents the copper from scaling, and causes the tin to be fixed wherever it touches. Lately, zinc has been proposed for lining vessels instead of tin, to avoid the ill consequences which have been unjustly apprehended.

To paint Sail Cloth, so as to make it Pliant, Durable, and Water-proof.

Grind ninety-six pounds of English ochre with boiled oil, and add to it sixteen pounds of black paint. Dissolve a pound of yellow soap in one pail of water on the fire, and mix it while hot with the paint. Lay this composition, without wetting it, upon the canvas, as stiff as can conveniently be done with the brush, so as to form a smooth surface; the next day, or the day after (if the latter so much the better), lay on a second coat of ochre and black, with a very little, if any, soap; allow this coat a day to dry, and then finish the canvas with black paint.

To make Oil-Cloth.

The manner of making oil-cloth, or, as the vulgar sometimes term it, *oil-skin*, was at one period a mystery. The process is now well understood, and is equally simple and useful.

Dissolve some good rosin or gum-lac over the fire in drying linseed oil, till the rosin is dissolved, and the oil brought to the thickness of a balsam. If this be spread upon canvas, or any other linen cloth, so as fully to drench and entirely to glaze it over, the cloth, if then suffered to dry thoroughly, will be quite impenetrable to wet of every description.*

* This preparation will likewise be found both useful and economical in securing timber from the effects of wet.

This varnish may either be worked by itself or with some colour added to it: as verdigris for a green; umber for a hair colour; white lead and lamp-black for a gray; indigo and white for a light blue, &c. To give the colour, you have only to grind it with the last coat of varnish you lay on. You must be as careful as possible to lay on the varnish equally in all parts.

A better method, however, of preparing oil-cloth is first to cover the cloth or canvas with a liquid paste, made with drying oil in the following manner: Take Spanish white or tobacco-pipe clay which has been completely cleaned by washing and sifting it from all impurities, and mix it up with boiled oil, to which a drying quality has been given by adding a dose of litharge one-fourth the weight of the oil. This mixture, being brought to the consistence of thin paste, is spread over the cloth or canvas by means of an iron spatula equal in length to the breadth of the cloth. When the first coating is dry, a second is applied. The unevennesses occasioned by the coarseness of the cloth or the unequal application of the paste are smoothed down with pumice-stone reduced to powder, and rubbed over the cloth with a bit of soft serge or cork dipped in water. When the last coating is dry, the cloth must be well washed in water to clean it; and, after it is dried, a varnish composed of gum-lac dissolved in linseed oil boiled with turpentine is applied to it, and the process is complete. The colour of the varnished cloth thus produced is yellow; but different tints can be given to it in the manner already pointed out.

An improved description of this article, intended for figured and printed varnished cloths, is obtained by using a finer paste, and cloth of a more delicate texture.

To prepare Varnished Silk.

Varnished silk, often employed for umbrellas, coverings to hats, &c., being impenetrable to wet, is prepared, and the operation performed, in the same manner as I have described in the second method of preparing oil cloth, but with a different kind of varnish or paste.

The paste used for silk is composed of linseed oil boiled with a fourth part of litharge; tobacco-pipe clay, dried and sifted, sixteen parts; litharge, ground on porphyry or very fine marble, and likewise dried and sifted, three parts; lamp-black one part. After the washing of the silk, fat copal varnish is applied instead of that used for oil-cloth.

To paint Cloth, Cambric, Sarcenet, &c., so as to render them Transparent.

Grind to a fine powder three pounds of clear white rosin, and put it into two pounds of good nut oil, to which a strong drying quality has been given; set the mixture over a moderate fire, and keep stirring it till all the rosin is dissolved; then put in two pounds of the best Venice turpentine, and keep stirring the whole well together; and, if the cloth or cambric be thoroughly varnished on both sides with this mixture, it will be quite transparent.

I should remark that, in this operation, as well as in the preparation of oil-cloths and varnished silks, the surfaces upon which the varnish or paste is to be applied must be stretched tight, and made fast during the application.

This mode of rendering cloth, &c. transparent is excellently adapted for window-blinds. The varnish will likewise admit of any design in oil colours being executed upon it as a transparency.

To thicken Linen Cloth for Screens.

Grind whiting with flowers of zinc, and add a little honey to it; then take a soft brush, and lay it upon the cloth, repeating the operation two or three times, and giving it time to dry between the different coatings. For the last coat, smooth it over with linseed oil nearly boiling, and mixed with a small quantity of the litharge of gold — the better to enable the cloth to stand the weather.

Printers' Ink.

Printers' ink is a real black paint, composed of lampblack, and linseed oil which has undergone a degree of heat superior to that of any of the common drying oils.

The manner of preparing it is extremely simple. Boil linseed oil in a large iron pot for eight hours, adding to it bits of toasted bread, for the purpose of absorbing the water contained in the oil. Let it rest till the following morning, and then expose it to the same degree of heat for eight hours more, or till it has acquired the consistence required; then add lamp-black worked up with a mixture of oil of turpentine and turpentine.

The consistence depends on the degree of heat given to the oil, and the quantity of lamp-black mixed up with it; and this consistence is regulated by the strength of the paper for which the ink is intended.

The preparation of printers' ink should take place in the open air, to prevent the bad effects arising from the vapour of the burnt oil, and, in particular, to guard against accidents by fire.

Sticking, or Court Plaster.

This plaster is well known from its general use and its healing properties. It is merely a kind of varnished silk, and its manufacture is very easy.

Bruise a sufficient quantity of isinglass, and let it soak in a little warm water for four-and-twenty hours; expose it to heat over the fire till the greater part of the water is dissipated, and supply its place by proof spirits of wine, which will combine with the isinglass. Strain the whole through a piece of open linen, taking care that the consistence of the mixture shall be such that, when cool, it may form a trembling jelly.

Extend the piece of black silk, of which you propose making your plaster, on a wooden frame, and fix it in that position by means of tacks or pack-thread. Then apply the isinglass (after it has been rendered liquid by a gentle heat) to the silk with a brush of fine hair (badger's is the best). As soon as this first coating is dried, which will not be long, apply a second; and afterwards, if you wish the article to be very superior, a third. When the whole is dry, cover it with two or three coatings of the balsam of Peru.

This is the genuine court plaster. It is pliable, and never breaks, which is far from being the case with many of the spurious articles which are sold under that name. Indeed, this commodity is very frequently adulterated. A kind of plaster, with a very thick and brittle covering, is often sold for it. The manufacturers of this, instead of isinglass, use common glue, which is much cheaper; and cover the whole with spirit varnish, instead of balsam of Peru. This plaster cracks, and has none of the balsamic smell by which the genuine court plaster is distinguished. Another method of detecting the adulteration is to moisten it with your tongue *on the side opposite to that which is varnished;* and, if the plaster be genuine, it will adhere exceedingly well. The adulterated plaster is too hard for this; it will not stick, unless you moisten it on the varnished side.

To imitate Tortoise-shell with Horn.

Mix up an equal quantity of quicklime and red lead with strong soap-lees; lay it on the horn with a small brush, in imitation of the mottle of tortoise-shell; when it is dry, repeat it two or three times.

Or, grind an ounce of litharge and half an ounce of quicklime together, with a sufficient quantity of liquid salt of tartar to make it of the consistence of paint. Put it on the horn with a brush, in imitation of tortoiseshell, and in three or four hours it will have produced the desired effect; it may then be washed off with clean water; if not deep enough, it may be repeated.

There is still another mode of effecting this imitation. Take a piece of lunar caustic, about the size of a pea, grind it with water on a stone, and mix with it a sufficient portion of gum-arabic to make it of a proper consistence, then apply it with a brush to the horn in imitation of the veins of tortoise-shell. A little red lead, or some other powder, mixed with it to give it a body, is of advantage. It will then stain the horn quite through, without hurting its texture and quality. In this case, however, you must be careful, when the horn is sufficiently stained, to let it be soaked for some hours in plain water, previous to finishing and polishing it.

A Varnish to preserve Glass from the Rays of the Sun.

Reduce a quantity of gum-tragacanth to fine powder, and let it dissolve for twenty-four hours in white of eggs well beat up; then rub it gently on the glass with a brush.

To imitate Rosewood.

Take half a pound of logwood, boil it with three pints of water till it is of a very dark red, to which add about half an ounce of salt of tartar; and, when boiling hot, stain your wood with two or three coats, taking care that it is nearly dry between each; then with a stiff flat brush, such as you use for graining, make streaks with a very deep black stain, which, if carefully executed, will be very near the appearance of dark rosewood.

The following is another method: Stain your wood all over with a black stain, and when dry, with a brush as above, dipped in the brightening liquid, form red veins in imitation of the grain of rosewood; which will produce, when well managed, a beautiful effect.

A handy brush for the purpose of veining may be made by taking a flat brush, such as you use for varnishing, and cutting the sharp points off the hairs, and making the edge irregular; by cutting out a few hairs here and there, you will have a tool which, without any trouble, will imitate the grain with great accuracy.

To imitate Black Rosewood.

The work must be grounded black; after which take some red lead well ground, and mixed up as before directed, which lay on with a flat stiff brush, in imitation of the streaks in the wood; then take a small quantity of lake, ground fine, and mix it with brown spirit-varnish, carefully observing not to have more colour in it than will just tinge the varnish; but should it happen, on trial, to be still too red, you may easily assist it with a little umber, ground very fine, or a small quantity of Vandyke-brown, which is better; with which pass over the whole of the work intended to imitate black rosewood, and it will have the desired effect: indeed, if well done, when it is varnished and polished, it will scarcely be known from rosewood.

A fine Black Varnish for Coaches and Iron Work.

Take two ounces of bitumen of Palestine, two ounces of rosin, and twelve ounces of umber; melt them separately, and afterwards mix them together over a moderate fire. Then pour upon them, while on the fire, six ounces of clear boiled linseed oil, and keep stirring the whole from time to time; take it off the fire, and, when pretty cool, pour in twelve ounces of the essence of turpentine.

A Varnish to imitate the Chinese.

Put four ounces of powdered gum-lac, with a piece of camphor about the size of a hazelnut, into a strong bottle, with a pound of good spirits of wine. Shake the bottle from time to time, and set it over some hot embers to mix for twenty-four hours, if it be in winter; in summer time, you may expose it to the sun. Pass the whole through a fine cloth, and throw away what remains upon it. Let it settle for twenty-four hours, and you will find a clear part in the upper part of the bottle, which you must separate gently, and put into another vial; and the remains will serve for the first layers or coatings.

To clean Silver Furniture.

Lay the furniture piece by piece upon a charcoal fire; and when they are just red, take them off and boil them in tartar and water, and your silver will have the same beauty as when first made.

To colour the Backs of Chimneys with Lead Ore.

Clean them with a very strong brush, and carefully rub off the dust and rust; pound about a quarter of a pound of lead ore into a fine powder, and put it into a vessel with half a pint of vinegar; then apply it to the back of the chimney with a brush. When it is made black with this liquid, take a dry brush, dip it in the same powder without vinegar, then dry and rub it with this brush, till it become as shining as glass.

To clean Marble, Sienna, Jasper, Porphyry, &c.

Mix up a quantity of the strongest soap-lees with quicklime, to the consistence of milk, and lay it on the stone, &c., for twenty-four hours; clean it afterwards with soap and water, and it will appear as new.

This may be improved by rubbing or polishing it afterwards with fine putty powder and olive oil.

A White for inside Painting, which in about four hours dries and leaves no smell.

Take one gallon of spirits of turpentine and two pounds of frankincense; let them simmer over a clear fire till dissolved, then strain and bottle it. Add one quart of this mixture to a gallon of bleached linseed oil, shake them well together, and bottle them likewise. Grind any quantity of white lead very fine with spirits of turpentine, then add a sufficient quantity of the last mixture to it till you find it fit for laying on. If it grows thick in working, it must be thinned with spirit of turpentine: it gives a flat or dead white.

To take Ink Spots out of Mahogany.

Apply spirits of salt with a rag, until the spot disappears, and immediately wash with clear water. Or, to half a pint of soft water put an ounce of oxalic acid, and half an ounce of butter of antimony; shake it well, and when dissolved it will be very useful for extracting stains out of mahogany, as well as ink, if not of too long standing.

To make Paste for Furniture.

Scrape four ounces of beeswax into a pot or basin; then add as much spirits of turpentine as will moisten it through; at the same time, pound a quarter of an ounce of rosin and add to it: when it is dissolved to the consistence of paste, add as much Indian red as will bring it to a deep mahogany colour: stir it up, and it is fit for use.

Another sort of paste may be made as follows:—

Scrape four ounces of beeswax as before; then take a pint of spirits of turpentine in a clean glazed pipkin, to which add an ounce of alkanet root; cover it close, and put it over a slow fire, attending it carefully, that it may not boil or catch fire; and when you perceive the colour to be drawn from the root, by the liquid being of a deep red, add as much of it to the wax as will moisten it through; at the same time, add a quarter of an ounce of powdered rosin, cover it close, and let it stand six hours, and it will be fit for use.

To make Oil for Furniture.

Take linseed oil; put it in a glazed pipkin, with as much alkanet root as it will cover; let it boil gently, and you will find it become of a strong red colour; let it cool, and it will be fit for use. Or, boil together cold drawn linseed oil and as much alkanet as it will cover, and to every quart of oil add two ounces of the best rose pink; when all the colour is extracted, strain it off, and for every quart add a gill of spirits of turpentine; it will be a very superior composition for soft and light mahogany.

To brown Gun Barrels.

Rub the barrel, after it is finished, with aqua-fortis, or spirit of salt diluted with water. Lay it by for a week till a complete coat is formed. Then apply a little oil, and after rubbing the surface dry, polish it with a hard, brush and a little beeswax.

To clean Pictures.

Having taken the picture out of its frame, take a clean towel, and, making it quite wet, lay it on the face of your picture, sprinkling it from time to time with clear soft water: let it remain wet for two or three days; take the cloth off, and renew it with a fresh one; after wiping your picture with a clean wet sponge, repeat the process till you find all the dirt soaked out of your picture; then wash it well with a soft sponge, and let it get quite dry; rub it with some clear nut or linseed oil, and it will look as well as when freshly done.

Another Method.

Put into two quarts of strong lye a quarter of a pound of Genoa soap rasped very fine, with about a pint of spirits of wine; let them simmer on the fire for half an hour, then strain them through a cloth; apply it with a brush to the picture, wipe it off with a sponge, and apply it a second time, which will effectually remove all dirt; then with a little nut oil warmed rub the picture, and let it dry; this will make it look as bright as when it came out of the artist's hands.

Varnish for Clock Faces, &c.

Take of spirits of wine one pint; divide it into four parts; mix one part with half an ounce of gum mastic, in a bottle by itself; one part of spirits and half an ounce of gum sandrac in another bottle; and one part of spirits and half an ounce of the whitest part of gum benjamin; mix and temper them to your mind; if too thick, add spirits; if too thin, some mastic; if too soft, some sandrac or benjamin. When you use it, warm the silvered plate before the fire, and with a flat camel-hair pencil stroke it over till no white streaks appear; which will preserve the silvering for many years.

Varnish for Balloons.

Take some linseed oil, rendered drying by boiling it with two ounces of sugar of lead and three ounces of litharge for every pint of oil till they are dissolved, which may be in half an hour. Then put a pound of birdlime and half a pint of the drying oil into an iron or copper vessel, whose capacity should equal about a gallon, and let it boil very gently over a slow charcoal fire, till the birdlime ceases to crackle, which will be in about half or three-quarters of an hour; then pour upon it two pints and a half more of the drying oil, and let it boil about an hour longer, stirring it frequently with an iron or wooden spatula. As the varnish, whilst boiling, and especially when nearly ready, swells very much, care should be taken to remove, in those cases, the pot from the fire, and to replace it when the varnish subsides; otherwise, it will boil over. Whilst the stuff is boiling, the operator should occasionally examine whether it has boiled enough, which may be known by observing whether, when rubbed between two knives, which are then to be separated from one another, the varnish forms threads between them, as it must then be removed from the fire. When nearly cool, add about an equal quantity of oil of turpentine. In using the varnish, the stuff must be stretched, and the varnish applied lukewarm. In twenty-four hours, it will dry.

As the elastic rosin, known by the name of Indian rubber, has been much extolled for a varnish for balloons, the following method of making it, as practiced by M. Blanchard, may not prove unacceptable: Dissolve elastic rosin cut small in five times its weight of rectified essential oil of turpentine, by keeping them some days together. Then boil one ounce of this solution in eight ounces of drying linseed oil for a few minutes; strain the solution, and use it warm.

DISEASES AND ACCIDENTS

TO WHICH PAINTERS AND VARNISHERS ARE PARTICULARLY LIABLE.

The business of a painter and varnisher is generally, and not without reason, considered an unhealthy one. Many of the substances which he is necessarily in the habit of employing are of a nature to do injury to the constitution; and great caution and care are required to prevent these from producing serious consequences. Much, however, of the mischief that is done arises from the want of proper precaution; the being ignorant of the symptoms of disorder, or want of due attention to them in the beginning; and, more than all, the use of improper remedies, from being unacquainted with those that ought to be used. I think, therefore, that I shall be rendering an acceptable service to the painter and varnisher by mentioning the principal diseases to which their occupations render them more liable than persons differently employed, with the proper means of remedies.

Painter's Colic.

This disease, the most common and the most dangerous to which painters are liable, arises with them from breathing in the fumes and handling the different preparations of white lead. It is a violent species of colic, and may be produced by other causes; but when it proceeds from lead it is always the most obstinate, and the most tedious and difficult of cure.

The first symptoms are a pain at the pit of the stomach, gradually increasing and proceeding downwards to the bowels; it is particularly violent round the navel. The person is likewise affected with frequent belching, slight sickness at the stomach, continued thirst, a quick short pulse, a confinement of the bowels, and repeated attempts to obtain a stool without effect.

When some or all of these symptoms are experienced, a strong dose of castor oil should be immediately taken and repeated till it opens the body freely. If it will not act, calomel pills must be taken in turn with the castor oil; and should both these fail to purge effectually, a clyster must also be employed, composed of ten ounces of senna and three grains of opium in solution. The warm bath as well as warm fomentations in flannel cloths of the lower part of the stomach are extremely serviceable in relieving the spasms; and should the symptoms continue, a blister applied to the abdomen may prove useful.

The person affected should be kept as quiet as possible both in body and mind: he should take no wine, spirits, malt liquor, nor any kind of solid food; but should confine himself to broth diet, and copious draughts of weak diluting drinks, such as barley-water.

Where the bowels are very obstinately confined, and the person is young and of a full habit, it may be advisable to begin with taking from him a quantity of blood, according to circumstances, in order to prevent inflammation.

I have not mentioned the strength of the doses to be employed as purgatives, because that must be determined by the constitution of the sick person and the manner in which the medicines operate. In a general way, remember never to give too strong a dose at once, as it can always be repeated as often as may be found necessary.

If the remedies I have mentioned prove successful in removing the early symptoms of the dry belly-ache, which will generally be the case, the person who has suffered, on returning to his work, should, if possible, entirely avoid, for some time, all parts of his business in which preparations of lead are employed. He should also, long after he may seem to feel quite well, keep to the light diet I have mentioned above, or he may bring on a relapse worse than the first attack of the disorder.

Few distempers grow more rapidly worse, and it is of the utmost importance to attend to its first symptoms, for if these are neglected, the most frightful consequences ensue. The violence of the pains increase beyond description; the outside of the belly feels pain at the slightest touch, and the muscles inside become wrapped into knots; a difficulty of making water, sometimes amounting to almost a total stoppage, takes place; and the bowels are so contracted by spasms as scarcely to admit a clyster. If these symptoms proceed, the spasms become more frequent and violent; and either the costiveness cannot be overcome (in which case inflammation in the bowels succeeds, and the patient's death is certain), or, if his life be saved, he generally remains a victim, in a greater or less degree, to the palsy.

I have mentioned these fatal circumstances to show the necessity of immediately attending to the first appearance of this dangerous disorder. In an advanced state of it, I do not pretend to prescribe—the best medical assistance must immediately be obtained. The remedies I have recommended are only designed for that early stage of the distemper for which the symptoms have already been described. They may then be used with advantage, and, if persevered in, will prevent the danger of severer suffering.

Weakness of the Wrists.

This is a partial kind of palsy, which sometimes remains after the painter's colic is cured. In some cases, too, it comes on without any previous attack of that disorder, where the injury has been more owing to handling lead than inhaling its fumes.

Where this weakness of the wrists is experienced by a painter, let him take, three or four times a-day, a dose of nitrate of silver, of from one to three grains, according to the manner in which it may operate. Before taking each of these doses, he should also take some castor oil. If it purge him too violently, let a little opium be mixed with the dose, lest bloody stools should be brought on. It is better to give the nitrate of silver in solution than in a solid form.

Where the bowels are so weak as to make any strong purge dangerous, this weakness of the wrists has often been cured by rubbing a drachm of strong mercurial ointment upon them every night and morning till the mouth became sore. Indeed, this will always be found a useful application.

One of the best methods in the weakness of the wrists arising from the handling of lead is, in addition to the taking of medicine or the application of mercurial ointment, to make use of a splint, made something like a battledore, fastened under the forearm, and continued to the extremities of the fingers. This has, in many instances, restored the strength of the wrists, even where the weakness amounted to complete palsy.

I have already observed that confirmed palsy may be the effect of a violent attack of the painter's colic. The remarks, however, which I made under that head apply here. I shall not venture to prescribe for that melancholy state of disease. My object is not to point out remedies for those extreme cases, but to suggest the best means of preventing them.

Effects of Poisonous Substances used in Painting and Varnishing.

These are principally lead, quicksilver, arsenic, and verdigris. Of the injurious effects of lead I have already spoken. Arsenic is found in some particular colours, especially in *orpiment* and *realgar;* and the circumstance is a strong objection to the use of them. Quicksilver enters into the composition of various amalgams employed in lacquering and gilding. The poisonous properties of verdigris are well known.

It cannot be too strongly impressed upon the mind of the painter or varnisher that mineral poisons of every description are as effectually taken into the system of the body by handling them, or inhaling their fumes, as by actually swallowing them; and that the consequences, though not so immediately fatal, are as certainly injurious. Care should therefore be taken not to handle them more than is absolutely necessary; and likewise, by keeping a thorough draft of air, and leaning as little as possible over such substances during their preparation, to avoid, as much as in your power, the breathing in the fumes arising from them.

But as you cannot entirely escape these, it will be well to know how to distinguish their respective characters. The effects of lead are sufficiently distinguished by the peculiar diseases it produces, which have been noticed before. Arsenic and quicksilver are attended with different consequences. When the former has found its way into the stomach, it will occasion a pricking and burning sensation, with thirst and sometimes vomiting. A pain will likewise be felt in the bowels, but without producing purging. If, after using colours which contain a mixture of arsenic, you experience any of these symptoms, a little fresh charcoal powdered fine, in small doses repeated, will be found very serviceable. An emetic should also be taken, and the body kept well open.

The fumes or handling of quicksilver produce, besides the symptoms mentioned in speaking of arsenic, salivation in a greater or less degree, bad breath, griping pains in the stomach, and severe purging. White of egg, dissolved in water and filtered, and diluted as circumstances require, is one of the best remedies when these symptoms are violent. A very good emetic, in such cases, is one ounce of sub-carbonate of magnesia dissolved in a pint of water; a glassfull of the mixture being taken every few minutes, at such intervals as are needful to promote vomiting.

Verdigris is readily distinguished by its nauseous and corroding effects upon the stomach. If you have reason to think you have suffered from the frequent use of this colour, common sugar, taken in such quantities as to open the bowels frequently, will be found the very best remedy.

I strongly recommend to every painter and varnisher, when engaged in any part of his business which requires him to employ a poisonous substance, whether lead or any other, the use of tobacco—I mean *chewing* it. It is the most powerful check to a substance acting to produce spasms by suspending the muscular action in the stomach. In short, tobacco possesses in this respect the advantages without the danger of opium, and has been found of the greatest service to persons in the trades above mentioned. At the same time, persons who use it for the purpose I have stated should be careful not to indulge in the practice too freely; for the excessive chewing of tobacco will not only occasion a feeling of stupid languor, which unfits a man for exertion, but may in time bring on a disease almost as much to be dreaded as the evils which it is intended to guard against.

Nausea.

Oil of turpentine, burnt oils of several descriptions, and some other substances used in painting and varnishing, give out fumes which, though not of a poisonous nature, are apt to occasion a slight sickness at the stomach, accompanied with a headache and a fainting sensation, to persons whose nerves are not strong: and these effects are frequently felt by young people before they become accustomed to the business. In many cases, removing for a short time from the offensive fumes into a pure air, and drinking a very little spring water, will dissipate these feelings. If they return, some opening medicine, or an emetic should be taken, which, if a foul stomach, as often happens, has been the cause, will remove it. But if you are a beginner in the business, and find yourself constantly affected in this manner on such occasions, I would advise you to turn to some other occupation; for a person of decidedly weak nerves will be subject to constant ill health as a painter.

Burns and Scalds.

In no business are these accidents more liable to occur to the persons engaged in it than in painting, varnishing, and gilding.

In all scalds and burns, it is of the first importance to

apply a remedy at the instant. Spirit of wine or turpentine, applied at the moment, generally prevent the rising of blisters; if it be rectified spirit, it is so much the better. Spirit of wine or turpentine is decidedly the best immediate remedy when the skin is broken. If the violence or size of the burns or scalds render the application of the spirit in the common way too painful, cover the injured parts with pieces of bladder softened by dipping them in warm water, and keep the outer surface constantly wetted with the spirit.

When the burn is considerable, fresh yolk of egg (if spirit is not at hand) applied to it will relieve the pain and forward the cure. A salve composed of one part of yellow wax and three parts of olive oil, which you can easily make yourself and carry about you in case of an accident, will likewise be extremely useful if applied at the moment of its happening.

Scraped potatoe is very often applied to a scald or burn. Some have pronounced it a certain cure, others have called it injurious: both parties are wrong. The fact is, it does nothing towards curing the burn; *but if applied at the first moment*, it prevents its becoming worse, and relieves the pain. It is therefore very right to apply it if no other remedy be near, till a better can be procured. Water, however, is almost always to be obtained, and, in the absence of other remedies, should instantly be had recourse to. The part or parts which have been injured should, without a moment's delay, be plunged into very cold water, or plentifully pumped upon, and an astonishingly rapid change from torture to ease will take place. After the immersion has continued a proper length of time, the parts injured should be covered with linen rags continually kept wetted with water and streams of air passed over them from time to time by a pair of bellows, till the person feels a freezing sensation.

Water is always serviceable in burns; and where the skin is not broken, many eminent surgeons consider it as the best of remedies.

GENERAL OBSERVATIONS.

I shall conclude this subject with a few general remarks principally respecting the diet and manner of living of the painter; on which, indeed, his exemption from the diseases which so severely affect many in his trade mainly depend.

He should avoid all acid drinks, such as cider and effervescing liquors; and abstain as much as possible from sours both in food and drink, even the use of vinegar; for acids have a particular tendency to combine with any portion of lead that he may have imbibed, and will act upon the stomach in a most injurious manner.

When a griping feeling is experienced by the painter, he often has recourse to a glass of raw spirits, with the idea of obtaining relief. Now, he cannot commit a greater error. This feeling indicates the commencement of that dangerous disorder the dry belly-ache, and spirituous liquors will both bring it on more rapidly and aggravate the symptoms. There is, besides, a vulgar but most mistaken notion that spirits taken inwardly are useful in guarding against the fumes of lead and other poisonous substances. And it is melancholy to see the number of persons engaged in the painting and varnishing line who, from this false idea, are led to adopt the pernicious practice of drinking drams in the morning;

and not unfrequently, from the hold this destructive habit gains upon them, at other times of the day too. Now, so far from this practice being serviceable, I can assure the dram-drinking painter that, whenever he is attacked by that disease so dangerous to those in his trade, he will find it rendered far more violent by his previous use of spirituous liquors and more likely to terminate in inflammation or palsy. Ardent spirits in a raw state should never be touched by the painter; and when taken mixed, they should rather be weak than otherwise.

I have had frequent occasion to observe that painters in general are partial to a great deal of solid and high-seasoned food. Now, it will be perceived that the disorder from which they have most to fear, and which is most common among them, is always attended by a confined state of the bowels from which its principal danger arises. A painter who regards his health should always prefer such food as is light and easy of digestion; and if he take any solids, it should be in small quantities, and not frequently. For the same reason, though I do not condemn malt liquor to a painter in good health, I should advise him not to take it in large quantities at a time, as it is heavy on the stomach. The lead which he cannot avoid more or less imbibing has a tendency to make him costive; and his business is not, like some others, accompanied with strong exercise to promote digestion.

I need scarcely remark on the advantages of cleanliness in his person to him, since the handling of preparations of lead is one of the injurious parts of his occupation.

In conclusion, let me once more impress upon him the importance and necessity of TEMPERANCE. The neglect of it in a workman of any other description *may* bring him to *sickness,* *must* bring him to *poverty;* but the intemperate and drunken Painter or Varnisher makes the most rapid strides in his power to bring upon himself painful sickness, and very often premature death.

THE END.

www.ingramcontent.com/pod-product-compliance
Lightning Source LLC
Chambersburg PA
CBHW031247290426
44109CB00012B/467